The Critical Moment

THE
CRITICAL
MOMENT

Essays
on the Nature
of
Literature

FABER AND FABER
24 Russell Square
London

First published in mcmlxiv
by Faber and Faber Limited
24 Russell Square, London, W.C.1
Printed in Great Britain by
Western Printing Services Ltd., Bristol

Contents

7

Introduction

━━━━━━━━━━━━━━◆⊃◦⊂◆━━━━━━━━━━━━━━

M an has so far had little success in changing the physical climates that he lives in. With climates of opinion he can sometimes do just a shade better. By printing, in its issues of 26 July and 27 September 1963, the essays to be found in this book, *The Times Literary Supplement* hoped to bring into more open and perhaps fruitful contact some of the very different climates of ideas in literary criticism that lie side by side, often without influencing each other at all, in Europe and America today.

The result, it will be seen, is a loud clash of concepts. English literary scholars and critics—and, in some spheres, their counterparts across the Atlantic—have held firm in late years to certain hard-headed ideas about the value of literature, and given short shrift to any others. But on the Continent many distinguished critics expound, with enthusiasm and eloquence, points of view that to the well-indoctrinated English student are likely to seem little short of disreputable. The right response to such a situation is surely neither to feel that the bulk of English criticism today is absurdly over-confident or one-sided; nor to suppose that England's thinkers, as ever, point the one way to reason, like Macaulay giving her credit for everything that was valuable in the European Enlightenment. The continental contributors to *The Critical Moment* can be seen as being in the same tight spot as their English and American counterparts—themselves fighting against what seem to be misleading, stultifying or simply distracting ways of thought, and holding on with an excessively tight grip to their own careful formulations.

In all debates such as this, in short, there is inevitably some hurling back and forth of refined and tested clichés. It does good on both sides. It will be noticed that several of the continental contributors to this volume—who wrote their essays partly in reply to those by the Anglo-Saxons—acknowledge the impact of American and English critical ideas, sometimes in a form not especially valued at home. *The Critical Moment* as a whole may perhaps strengthen this impact and lend some weight to the influence flowing in the other direction as well.

All the English contributors are or have been university teachers of English literature. This reflects clearly the way in which, over the past thirty or forty years, English literary criticism has become pretty solidly professional and specialized. Critics tend to plough more and more intensively ever smaller fields—so that a given critic may be a poetry man or a novel man, a Victorian or a Renaissance man, a Dickens man or a Henry James man, and, narrowing it down, perhaps an early Henry James or a late Dickens man. However, our English contributors here do not provide a spectacle of this sort. On the contrary, there is a striking and almost unanimous insistence in their essays on the larger aims of literature. They all belong in their different degrees to a tradition stemming, a century back, from Matthew Arnold, and more immediately from a striking coalescence of the ideas of Mr. T. S. Eliot, Professor I. A. Richards, and Dr. F. R. Leavis.

It would not be difficult to show, even from Mr. Eliot's earliest and most seminal essays, that he has expressed views of literature frankly stressing its power to give us intellectual and sensuous experiences quite different from those that come to us when we are pursuing our ordinary, everyday concerns. It is this 'aestheticism', indeed, that critics like Professor Yvor Winters have reproached him with, concerned as they are to stress the essentially rational and cognitive purpose of the greatest writing. But many English readers, on making acquaintance with Mr. Winters's opinions, have wondered at first if they were reading about the same Mr. Eliot. For what has penetrated deepest into English critical thought is Mr. Eliot's almost casual association of the poet's organizing power, in writers like Donne and Marvell, with *maturity*: maturity to an exceptionally developed degree, but in a sense not essentially different from that in which enlightened educationists—or even magistrates—use it today. How much importance Mr. Eliot attached to this rough equation is now difficult to say. But it has had an extraordinarily deep effect on his English followers.

Moreover, the kind of attention to the texture of literature which Mr. Eliot recommended—but only practised himself in rare passages of great brilliance—has constantly been used to an end deriving from just this view. 'Stylistics' as it has developed on the Continent, and to some extent in America, has never been in vogue in England. The details of the word-play of poets and novelists have been scrutinized above all with the aim of seeing whether they reflected—with the special force we hope for from our mentors—the qualities associated with 'maturity' in the sense mentioned: a real awareness of the variety and 'awkwardness' of the world, ability to plumb other people's feelings, a deep, impassioned purposefulness, and the capacity to direct all the emotions derived from these powers in an ultimately loving and rational way.

Professor Richards's general conception of literature working as a sort of psychic tonic has never taken much hold. It seemed much more significant from the start that the works he recommended in the nineteen-twenties were almost all the same ones as were praised by Mr. Eliot. His idea of poetry 'organizing our impulses' could be that much more easily assimilated to Mr. Eliot's notion of the poet's 'maturity' as their tastes were obviously so similar! As for Dr. Leavis, he has identified the writer's ability to present his material with his degree of moral development in a quite explicit way, and has been the most direct influence of all.

Dr. Leavis's contribution to the present volume takes the specific form of a plea for preserving the highest standards in post-graduate research in English; and by 'the highest standards' he means not—as he would say—the empty academic demand that Ph.D. research should be a 'contribution to knowledge', but rather the requirement that the student should be called on to show genuine powers of perception, judgment and responsibility. Behind this plea lies Dr. Leavis's long-cherished vision of English literature as playing the role of 'central humanity' in a civilized education, and his belief that it calls for 'maturity' in turn from those teachers and critics who are going to speak or write about it.

Mr. Richard Hoggart, Mr. John Wain and Mr. W. W. Robson all take a view broadly similar to Dr. Leavis's. Mr. Hoggart sees literature as serving the task of enlarging our sympathy with individual suffering and joy, of extending our humanity. Without showing any overt moral designs on us, he says, it healthily subverts our view of life, working against 'fear, ambition, fatigue and laziness'. Mr. Wain puts a largely identical case in a different way when he deplores people 'using'— by which he implies 'abusing'—literature, as a means of wish-fulfilment; for him too the good critic works with the author in helping the reader to break out of his egotism, and see 'mysterious other people' as real individuals with real claims on life. Mr. Robson would like to have the word 'sincere' restored to the critical vocabulary, believing that it is only when a writer has genuinely lived in imagination through the experiences his work is concerned with that it can achieve the 'compassionate intelligence' and 'fine moral poise' found in great literature. All these three critics are quick to recognize that the kind of moral realism they admire in literature does not necessarily depend on any simple kind of realism in the stylistic sense. 'The truest poetry is the most feigning', quotes Mr. Wain. But, without going into detail, they all insist that the 'feigning' has a core of literal relevance to real human stituations; whatever Falstaff is, says Mr. Robson dryly, he is not a thin man.

Professor L. C. Knights has also long been known as a colleague of Dr. Leavis's, but in his essay here he lays more stress than the others—in a rather Coleridgean way—on the need for literature to awaken the imagination. He wants now to stress the importance of the immediate, intuitive response to literature. But he too looks beyond this awakening to its ultimate effect on the intimate personal life of the reader. It is Professor Graham Hough who hints most clearly at a fresh way in which English critical thought could develop, by recalling literature's power to give its readers not only a finer sense of realism, but also living myths, by which to guide their daily lives. (He is, not surprisingly, less attracted by the novel than any of the other English contributors seem to be.)

Of the American contributors, Mr. George Steiner strikes a rather more sceptical note. Looking at recent history, he wonders if men necessarily progress in love and wisdom through reading literature, however deeply those qualities pervade the literature in question. Nevertheless for him again literature achieves its ideal aim in adding to 'the knowledge or governance of human possibility'. Professor René Wellek and Professor Harry Levin are doubtless the most guarded of the Anglo-Saxon contributors to this book. Both are experts in Comparative Literature: Professor Wellek looks to the possibility of an overall theory which will take into account all the characteristics of literature that mark it off as a distinctive, autonomous phenomenon, without undermining the ultimate need to make a frank value-judgment on its human worth; Professor Levin, just as aware of this double task facing the critic, is drawn to a relaxed and sensitive eclecticism.

When they read 'Time and the Poetic Imagination' by Professor Emil Staiger, any readers who take for granted the prevailing English view of literature are evidently in for a shock. Of all the contributors to *The Critical Moment*, it is Professor Staiger who expresses most uncompromisingly an interest in literature utterly remote from those of most Anglo-Saxon critics. If we may, to make the point, compare a literary work with another work of human hands, a town, most Anglo-

Saxon critics are like men going about the streets inquiring in what ways the planning of the town enhances the daily life of the inhabitants—opens up new scope for them, offers means of sociability and pleasure, encourages them in noble ways of living. Professor Staiger is like a man quietly betaking himself, meanwhile, to a hillside outside the town and sitting down to look at it in the sunlight. The critics below may expostulate that that is not what the town was built for, that this is a complete dereliction of duty; the town-planners, in this case, are silent about their intentions; he goes on sitting there, indifferent to reproach, contented to take in the beauty of the town from where he sits and to begin to define—by looking more closely —what it is in what he sees that gives him his joyful sensations.

His tentative conclusions are that the main source of his delight is a sense of the 'unity' of the works in question, and that this unity comes from a consistent attitude to time on the writer's part that appears in every detail of substance or manner in the work. These of course are ways of thinking that open up quite different perspectives again, and challenge opposition on ground that is very indeterminate and shaky. But those critics who see art's essential value as being, on the highest level, educational, are cut off by their basic assumptions from any further consideration of the ideas that Professor Staiger raises.

In Italy and Spain, respectively, Professor Emilio Cecchi and Professor Dámaso Alonso are fighting somewhat similar battles to that which Professor Staiger is consciously waging against the main German tradition—all three of them being opposed to the study of literature as mere historical and psychological documentation. Signor Cecchi, while admiring Anglo-Saxon urbanity, also carries the war into our camp, finding the didactic stress of the Anglo-Saxon contributors to *The Critical Moment* overdone. Señor Alonso, while extremely interested in 'stylistics', nevertheless sees it as an 'imperfect science', of only secondary interest to the intuitive delight in literature which we start with.

'Stylistics', however, greatly concerns most of the other contributors. M. Raymond Picard, he too at odds with the prevailing French emphasis on the biography or psychology of writers, sees the Anglo-Saxon critics as his best allies in his insistence on the need for concentrating on the text. Perhaps he is over-generous here, if it is true that since Professor Richards's early work the main interest in the working of literary language, in England at least, has been in strict connexion with an interest in its social and moral value.

For a refined and subtle account of one way in which literary language may be approached, however, we may turn to 'Criticism as Language' by M. Roland Barthes. M. Barthes is not especially concerned with value; he is very concerned with the peculiar semantic systems constituted by poems and novels, and with the logical elucidation of them—which for him is no final activity, but the constantly renewed relating of those systems to the other systematic ways of describing our experience that intellectual changes continually reimpose on us. For him, therefore, criticism is a very relativistic affair, 'the dialogue between two historical situations and two subjectivities, those of the author and the critic'; the one thing that should characterize it in all its manifestations being the same stringent concern for logic in the dialogue. This point of view relates him fairly closely to the other Italian contributor, Signor Umberto Eco. Signor Eco singles out Professor Richards, with his interest in semantics, as the English critic who has most stimulated him; it is 'poetics', the mechanism of communication in literature, that intrigues him most of all, especially, as he wittily remarks, in an age when complex works more and more contain their own theorizing about the problem, at which rate research into poetics will soon be the only possible form of criticism.

Professor Jan Kott, of Warsaw University, gives one more vivid impression of ideas growing and clashing in a society different from ours. It is pleasant to see unexpected names, like those of Newman and Chesterton, and Gordon Craig, respected as refreshing influences at different points in fairly recent Polish cultural history. But it is particularly interesting to read that in Poland, too, the younger critics and scholars have turned above all for guidance to one of the great thinkers about poetic structure and communication theory, the Russian Professor Roman Jakobson of Harvard University. Professor Jakobson's name, and that of de Saussure, the head of the earlier Geneva school which opened up these problems, are two names that are quoted repeatedly in the continental half of this symposium—both of them thinkers who have had little following in England.

Perhaps it is Professor Hans Mayer, until recently at Leipzig, who will seem to speak with a voice most like the English critics. Professor Mayer probably owes more to Marxist thought than any of the other writers in *The Critical Moment*, though scorning any naive linking of the forms literature takes with its social background. Nor is his evaluation of literary works based on any simple sense of their social value. Nevertheless the 'function' of the work, its degree of fairly direct 'usefulness' to its readers, weighs heavier with him than with any of the other continental critics in the book. From his own starting-point he seems to have reached—if we may use the phrase—a sort of 'higher populism' not so very far removed from the mainstream of critical thought in England today.

All in all, then, readers of this volume may feel inclined to recognize that both in its assumptions about the value of literature, and in its understanding of literary form, English criticism at present is more closed and unadventurous than it should be. At the same time, though, we English may feel an impulse to come back against the charge of over-didacticism with the thought that criticism on the Continent falls under strong suspicion of being academic *without* even being didactic: that in its attention to the more esoteric values of literature, or to purely logical study of poetic structure, it does not go very far in answering the demands that in practice most readers make upon critics and teachers—namely to guide them, with real attention to their needs, to the reading that will be most valuable to them. Some such poise, between confidence in what has so far been done and willingness to consider further what has not, seems to be most desirable for English criticism now.

Some perception of the truth, some shaft of valuable insight, is always likely to enlighten the work of any serious and devoted critic, no matter how different the basic assumptions of his thought from those of his neighbour. The great cabbalist of Anatole France's *La Rôtisserie de la Reine Pédauque*, M. d'Astarac, was convinced that the story of the Fall in the Old Testament must be taken symbolically, because if Adam and Eve had eaten a real apple, God, with his unfailing sense of the appropriate, would have punished them with eternal indigestion. In a world of imperfect understanding M. d'Astarac will perhaps always be the type of the really worth-while critic: nobly speculative, liable to disastrous errors in his exalted reasoning, yet falling from time to time with perfect instinct on the truth.

Part I

GEORGE STEINER

Humane Literacy

⬛⬛⬛◦⟩⊃∘⊂⟨◦⬛⬛⬛

W hen he looks back, the critic sees a eunuch's shadow. Who would be a critic if he could be a writer? Who would hammer out the subtlest insight into Dosto- evsky if he could weld an inch of the Karamazovs, or argue the poise of Lawrence if he could shape the free gust of life in *The Rainbow*? All great writing springs from *le dur désir de durer*, the harsh contrivance of spirit against death, the hope to overreach time by force of creation. 'Brightness falls from the air'; five words and a trick of darkening sound. But they have outworn three centuries. Who would choose to be a literary critic if he could set verse to sing, or compose, out of his own mortal being, a vital fiction, a character that will endure? Most men have their dusty survivance in old telephone directories (it is a mercy that these are kept at the British Museum); there is in the literal fact of their existence, less of life's truth and harvest than in Falstaff or Mme de Guermantes. To have imagined these.

The critic lives at second-hand. He writes *about*. The poem, the novel or the play must be given to him; criticism exists by the grace of other men's genius. By virtue of style, criticism can itself become literature. But usually this occurs only when the writer is acting as critic of his own work or as outrider to his own poetics, when the criticism of Coleridge is work in progress or that of T. S. Eliot propaganda. Is there anyone but Sainte- Beuve who belongs to literature purely as a critic? It is not criticism that makes the language live.

These are simple truths (and the honest critic says them to

21

himself in the grey of morning). But we are in danger of forgetting them, because the present time is peculiarly charged with autonomous critical energy and prestige. Critical journals pour out a deluge of commentary or exegesis; in America there are schools of criticism. The critic exists as a persona in his own right; his persuasions and quarrels have a public role. Critics write about critics, and the bright young man, instead of regarding criticism as defeat, as a gradual, bleak coming to terms with the ash and grit of one's limited talent, thinks of it as a career of high note. This would merely be funny; but it has a corrosive effect. As never before, the student and the person interested in the current of literature reads reviews and critiques of books rather than the books themselves, or before he has made the effort of personal judgment. Dr. Leavis's statement of the maturity and intelligence of George Eliot is part of the common coin of present feeling. How many of those who can echo it have actually read *Felix Holt* or *Daniel Deronda*? Mr. Eliot's essay on Dante is a commonplace in literary education; the *Commedia* is known, if at all, in a few brief excerpts (*Inferno* XXVI or Ugolino famished). The true critic is servant to the poet; today he is acting as master, or being taken as such. He omits Zarathustra's last, most vital lesson: 'now, do without me.'

Precisely one hundred years ago, Matthew Arnold saw a similar breadth and salience of critical impulse. He recognized that this impulse was secondary to that of the writer, that the joy and importance of creation were of a radically higher order. But he regarded the period of critical bustle as a necessary prelude to a new poetic age. We come *after*, and that is the nerve of our condition. After the unprecedented ruin of humane values and hopes by the political bestiality of our age.

That ruin is the starting-point of any serious thought about literature and the place of literature in society. Literature deals essentially and continually with the image of man, with the shape and motive of human conduct. We cannot act now, be it as critics or merely as rational beings, as if nothing of vital relevance had happened to our sense of the human possibility, as if the extermination by hunger or violence of some 70 million men, women and children in Europe and Russia between 1914 and 1945 had not altered, profoundly, the quality of our awareness. We cannot pretend that Belsen is irrelevant to the responsible life of the imagination. What man has wrought on man, in very recent time, has affected the writer's primary material—the sum and potential of human behaviour—and it presses on the brain with a new darkness.

Moreover, it puts in question the primary concepts of a literary, humanistic culture. The ultimate of political barbarism grew from the core of Europe. Two centuries after Voltaire had proclaimed its end, torture again became a normal process of political action. Not only did the general dissemination of literary, cultural values prove no barrier to totalitarianism; but in notable instances the high places of humanistic learning and art actually welcomed and aided the new terror. Barbarism prevailed on the very ground of Christian humanism, of Renaissance culture and classic rationalism. We know that some of the men who devised and administered Auschwitz had been trained to read Shakespeare or Goethe, and continued to do so.

This is of obvious and appalling relevance to the study or teaching of literature. It compels us to ask whether knowledge of the best that has been thought and said does, as Matthew Arnold asserted, broaden and refine the resources of the human spirit. It forces us to wonder whether what Dr. Leavis has called 'the central humanity' does, in fact, educate toward humane action, or whether there is not between the tenor of moral intelligence developed in the study of literature and that required in social and political choice, a wide gap or contrariety. The latter possibility is particularly disturbing. There is some evidence that a trained, persistent commitment to the life of the printed word, a capacity to identify deeply and critically with imaginary personages or sentiments, diminishes the immediacy, the hard edge of actual circumstance. We come to respond more acutely to the literary sorrow than to the misery next door. Here also recent times give harsh evidence. Men who wept at Werther or Chopin moved, unrealizing, through literal hell.

This means that whoever teaches or interprets literature—and both are exercises seeking to build for the writer a body of living, discerning response—must ask of himself what he is about (to tutor, to guide someone through *Lear* or the *Oresteia* is to take into one's hand the quick of his being). Assumptions regarding the value of literate culture to the moral perception of the individual and society were self-evident to Johnson, Coleridge and Arnold. They are now in doubt. We must countenance the possibility that the study and transmission of literature may be of only marginal significance, a passionate luxury like the preservation of the antique. Or, at worst, that it may detract from more urgent and responsible uses of time and energy of spirit. I do not believe either to be true. But the question must be asked and explored without cant. Nothing is more worrying regarding the present state of English studies in the universities than the fact that such inquiry should be deemed bizarre or subversive. It is of the essence.

This is where the claim of the natural sciences derives its force. Pointing to their criteria of empirical verification and to their tradition of collaborative achievement (in contrast to the apparent idiosyncrasy and egotism of literary argument), scientists have been tempted to assert that their own methods and vision are now at the centre of civilization, that the ancient primacy of poetic statement and metaphysical image is over. And though the evidence is uncertain, it does seem likely that of the aggregate of available talent, many, and many of the best, have turned to the sciences. In the *quattrocento* one would have wished to know the painters; today, the sense of inspired joy, of the mind in free, unshadowed play, is with the physicists, the biochemists and the mathematicians.

But we must not be deceived. The sciences will enrich language and the resources of feeling (as Thomas Mann showed in *Felix Krull*, it is from astrophysics and microbiology that we may reap our future myths, the terms of our metaphors). The

24

sciences will recast our surroundings and the context of leisure or subsistence in which culture is viable. But though they are of inexhaustible fascination and frequent beauty, the natural and mathematical sciences are only rarely of ultimate interest. I mean that they have added little to our knowledge or governance of human possibility, that there is demonstrably more of insight into the matter of man in Homer, Shakespeare or Dostoevsky than in the entirety of neurology or statistics. No discovery of genetics impairs or surpasses what Proust knew of the spell or burden of lineage; each time Othello reminds us of the rust of dew on the bright blade we experience more of the sensual, transient reality in which our lives must pass than it is the business or ambition of physics to impart. No sociometry of political motive or tactics weighs a feather against Stendhal.

And it is precisely the 'objectivity', the moral neutrality in which the sciences rejoice and attain their brilliant community of effort, that bar them from final relevance. Science may have given tools and insane pretences of rationality to those who devised mass murder. It tells us scarcely anything of their motives, a topic on which Aeschylus or Dante would be worth hearing. Nor, to judge by the naive political statements put forward by our present alchemists, can it do much to make the future less vulnerable to the inhuman. What light we possess on our essential, inward condition is still gathered by the poet.

But, undeniably, many parts of the mirror are today cracked or blurred. The dominant characteristic of the present literary scene is the excellence of 'non-fiction'—of reportage, history, philosophic argument, biography, the critical essay—over traditional imaginative forms. Most of the novels, poems and plays produced in the past two decades are simply not as well written, not as strongly felt, as are modes of writing in which the imagination obeys the impulse of fact. Madame de Beauvoir's memoirs are what her novels should have been, marvels of physical and psychological immediacy; Edmund Wilson writes the best prose in America; none of the numerous novels or poems that have taken on the dread theme of the concentration camps rivals the truth, the controlled poetic mercy of Bettelheim's factual analysis, *The Informed Heart*. It is as if the complication, pace, and political enormity of our age had bewildered and driven back the confident master-builder's imagination of classic literature and the nineteenth-century novel. A novel by Butor and *Naked Lunch* are both escapes. The avoidance of the major human note, or the derision of that note through erotic and sadistic fantasy, points to the same failure of creation. Monsieur Beckett is moving, with unflinching Irish logic, toward a form of drama in which a character, his feet trapped in concrete and his mouth gagged, will stare at the audience and say nothing. The imagination has supped its fill of horrors and of the unceremonious trivia through which modern horror is often expressed. As rarely before, poetry is tempted by silence.

It is in this context of privation and uncertitude that criticism has its modest yet vital place. Its function is, I believe, threefold.

First, it may show us what to re-read, and how. The sum of literature is obviously immense, and the pressure of the new constant. One must choose, and in that choice criticism has its use. This does not mean that it should play the role of destiny and single out a handful of authors or works as the only valid tradition, excluding others (the mark of good criticism is that it opens more books than it closes). It means that from the vast, entangled legacy of the past, criticism will bring to light and sustain that which speaks to the present with particular directness or exaction.

This is the proper distinction between the critic and the historian of literature or philologist. To the latter the value of a text is intrinsic; it has a linguistic or chronological fascination independent of larger relevance. The critic, while availing himself of the scholar's authority on the primary meaning and integrity of the work, must choose. And his bias will be toward that which enters into dialogue with the living.

Each generation makes its choice. There is permanent poetry but hardly any permanent criticism. Tennyson shall have his day, and Donne his eclipse. Or to give an instance less dependent on the play of fashion: before the war, it was commonplace in the French lycées in which I was educated to consider Virgil as a fussy, nerveless imitator of Homer. Any boy would tell you so with cool assurance. With disaster, and the routine of flight and exile, this view changed radically. Virgil now seemed the more mature, the more necessary witness (Simone Weil's perverse reading of the *Iliad*, and Hermann Broch's *Death of Virgil* are both part of this revaluation). Time, both historically and on the scale of personal life, alters our view of a work or body of art. There is, notoriously, a poetry of the young, and a prose of the aged. Because their trumpetings of a golden future contrast, ironically, with our actual experience, the romantics have moved out of focus. The sixteenth and early seventeenth centuries, though their language is often remote and intricate, seem nearer to our speech. Criticism can make these changes of need fruitful and discriminating. It can summon from the past what the genius of the present draws upon (the best of French prose at the moment has behind it the sinew of Diderot). And it can remind us that our alternances of judgment are neither axiomatic nor of lasting validity. The great critic will 'feel ahead'; he will lean over the horizon and prepare the context of future recognition. At times he hears the echo when the voice is forgotten, or before it is known. There were those who sensed, in the 1920s, that the time of Blake and Kierkegaard was at hand, or who discerned, ten years later, the general truth in the private nightmare of Kafka. This does not mean choosing winners; it means knowing there is a race on.

Secondly, criticism can relate. In an age in which rapidity of technical communication in fact conceals obstinate ideological and political barriers, the critic can act as intermediary and custodian. It is part of his job to see that a political regime cannot visit oblivion or distortion on the work of a writer, that of books burnt the ash is gathered and deciphered.

Even as he seeks to establish the dialogue between past and present, so the critic will try to keep open the lines of contact between languages. Criticism widens and complicates the map of sensibility. It insists that literatures do not live in isolation, but in a manifold of linguistic and national encounters. Criticism delights in affinity and the far leap of example. It knows that the incitements of a major talent or poetic form spread outward in intricate patterns of diffusion. It works 'à l'ensigne de Saint-Jérôme', knowing that there are no exact equivalences between languages, only betrayals, but that the attempt to translate is a constant need if the poem is to achieve its full life. Both critic and translator strive to communicate discovery.

In practice, this means that literature should be taught and interpreted in a comparative way. To have no direct acquaintance with the Italian epic when judging Spenser, to value Pope without a sure grasp of Boileau, to consider the performance of the Victorian novel and of James without a close awareness of Balzac, Stendhal, Flaubert, is to read thinly or falsely. It is academic feudalism that draws sharp lines between the study of English and of Modern Languages. Is English not a modern language, vulnerable and resilient, at all points in its history, to the pressure of European vernaculars and of the European tradition of rhetoric and genre? But the question cuts deeper than academic discipline. The critic who declares that a man can know only one language well, that the national inheritance of poetry or the national tradition of the novel is alone valid or supreme, is closing doors where they should be opened, is narrowing the mind where it should be brought to the sense of a large and equal achievement. Chauvinism has cried havoc in politics; it has no place in literature. The critic (and here again he differs from the writer) is not a man to stay in his own garden.

The third function of criticism is the most important. It concerns the judgment of contemporary literature. There is a distinction between contemporary and immediate. The immediate hounds the reviewer. But plainly, the critic has special responsibilities towards the art of his own age. He must ask of it not only whether it represents a technical advance or refinement, whether it adds a twist of style or plays adroitly on the nerve of the moment, but what it contributes to or detracts from the dwindled reserves of moral intelligence. What is the measure of man this work proposes? It is not a question which is easily formulated, or which can be put with unfailing tact. But our time is not of the ordinary. It labours under the stress of inhumanity, experienced on a scale of singular magnitude and horror; and the possibility of ruin is not far off. There are luxuries of detachment one should like to afford, but cannot.

This would, for example, lead one to ask whether the talent of Tennessee Williams is being used to purvey a mawkish sadism, whether the rococo virtuosity of Salinger is arguing an absurdly diminished and enervating view of human existence. It would lead one to ask whether the banality of Camus's plays, and of all but the first of his novels, does not connote the persistent vagueness, the statuesque but airy motion of his thought. To *ask*; not to mock or censor. The distinction is immensely important. The asking can only be fruitful where access to the work is wholly free, where the critic genuinely hopes for disagreement and counterstatement. Moreover, while the policeman or the censor asks of the writer, the critic asks only of the book.

What I have been aiming at, throughout, is the notion of *humane literacy*. In that great discourse with the living dead which we call reading, our role is not a passive one. Where it is more than reverie or an indifferent appetite sprung of boredom, reading is a mode of action. We engage the presence, the voice of the book. We allow it entry, though not unguarded, into our inmost. A great poem, a classic novel, press in upon us; they assail and occupy the strong places of our consciousness. They exercise upon our imagination and desires, upon our ambitions and most covert dreams, a strange, bruising mastery. Men who burn books know what they are doing. The artist is the uncontrollable force: no western eye, since Van Gogh, looks on a poplar without observing in it the start of flame.

So, and in supreme measure, it is with literature. A man who has read Book XXIV of the *Iliad*—the night meeting of Priam and Achilles—or the chapter in which Alyosha Karamazov kneels to the stars, who has read Montaigne's chapter XX (*Que philosopher c'est apprendre l'art de mourir*) and Hamlet's use of it—and who is not altered, whose apprehension of his own life is unchanged, who does not, in some subtle yet radical manner, look on the room in which he moves, on those that knock at the door, differently—has read only with the blindness of physical sight. Can one read *Anna Karenina* or Proust without experiencing a new infirmity or occasion in the very core of one's sexual feelings?

To read well is to take great risks. It is to make vulnerable our identity, our self-possession. In the early stages of epilepsy there occurs a characteristic dream (Dostoevsky tells of it). One is somehow lifted free of one's own body; looking back, one sees oneself and feels a sudden, maddening fear; another presence is entering into one's own person, and there is no avenue of return. Feeling this fear, the mind gropes to a sharp awakening. So it should be when we take in hand a major work of literature or philosophy, of imagination or doctrine. It may come to possess us so completely that we go, for a spell, in fear of ourselves and in imperfect recognition. He who has read Kakfa's *Metamorphosis* and can look into his mirror unflinching may technically be able to read print, but is illiterate in the only sense that matters.

Because the community of traditional values is splintered, because words themselves have been twisted and cheapened, because the classic forms of statement and metaphor are yielding to complex, transitional modes, the art of reading, of true literacy, must be reconstituted. It is the task of literary criticism to help us read as total human beings, by example of precision, fear, and delight. Compared to the act of creation, that task is secondary. But it has never counted more. Without it, creation itself may fall upon silence.

RICHARD HOGGART

Why I Value Literature

———————◆✑◦✑◆———————

It would be easier to write about why I like literature (or even about what I think literary criticism should do). 'Why I *value* literature' seems more precise, but its implications are wider and deeper. I shall start with the most comprehensive statement I can frame.

I value literature because of the way—the peculiar way—in which it explores, re-creates and seeks meaning in human experience. I value it because it explores the diversity, complexity and strangeness of that experience (of individual men or of men in groups or of man in relation to the natural world); because it re-creates the texture of that experience; because it pursues this exploration with a disinterested passion (not wooing nor apologizing nor bullying). I value literature, in short, because in it men look at life with all the vulnerability, honesty, and penetration they can command . . . and dramatize their insights by means of a unique relationship with language.

'Exploring human experience' is a useful phrase, but not quite sufficient on two counts. It is too active. 'Contemplating' or 'celebrating' human experience might be better for a beginning, to indicate the preoccupied passivity before life in which the imagination often starts its work. And 'exploring' can sound too much like a wandering for its own sake, as though literature simply opens up successive territories of human response. 'Searching' or even 'ordering' would be better, so long as we didn't imply by either of them an 'irritable reaching after fact and reason'. Every writer—not necessarily in an

31

obvious sense nor necessarily consciously, and whether in a tragic or a comic or in any other manner—means what he says. Sometimes he will deny that there is a meaning. 'I only wanted to write an interesting tale', he will say, forgetting that the interest of a story almost always comes from seeing the human will in action—against chaos or against order. Sometimes the meaning he intends will not be the work's real, its achieved, meaning. The ebb and flow of his imaginative power within the work may reveal attitudes and assumptions hidden from the writer himself; 'Never trust the teller; trust the tale.' But in all circumstances there will be a meaning, a kind of order—expressed or implied. Whether he knows it or not, the writer will be testing the validity of a certain way of seeing and of responding to life; he will be offering, no matter how provisionally, a way of ordering the flux of experience. By his choice and arrangement of materials, by the temper of his treatment of them, a writer is implicitly saying: this is how one man thinks we should face experience or succumb to it or seek to alter it or try to ignore it.

The attention good literature pays to life is both loving and strict. It frames experience and, in a sense, distances it. But it always assumes the importance, the worthwhileness, of human experience even when—as in tragedy—it finds much in that experience evil. So, if a writer is imaginatively gifted, his work helps both to define and to assert that importance, to bring experience up fresh before us. This is not to say that a good writer makes an evil experience good. But his exploration is good, since it defines more clearly the nature of the evil we suffer and perform. It helps to make us believe more in (say) the freely willing nature of man; and it helps us to feel more sharply the difficulties and the limits of that freedom. Good literature insists on 'the mass and majesty' of the world—on both its concreteness and sensuous reality, and on its meanings beyond mere 'thisness'. It insists too on the importance of the inner, the distinctive and individual, life of man, while much else in our activity and in our make-up—fear, ambition, fatigue, laziness—

seeks to make that life generalized and typecast. Literature assumes the truth of George Eliot's conviction that 'our moral progress may be measured by the degree in which we sympathize with *individual* suffering and *individual* joy'.

Of course, not all writing acts in this way. Roughly, we can say that there are two kinds of literature: conventional literature and live literature. This distinction cuts across the common divisions by brows. Conventional literature usually (it may sometimes do better than its author knows) reinforces existing assumptions, an individual's or a group's ways of looking at the world. Properly read, live literature—even the quietest or most light-hearted—may be very disturbing indeed, may deeply subvert our view of life.

'Properly read' is the key-phrase in that last sentence. I said at the beginning that literature explores, re-creates and orders human experience in a *unique* way. Other activities of the human mind and imagination explore human experience, and some re-create it, and some seek to order it. One can think here of philosophers or theologians or, just as relevantly, of composers or painters. I am not at all concerned to set literature against any of those. Literature can be, and often is, discursive in the way that some philosophy is; it has, like painting and music but unlike philosophy, an imaginative architectonic. Its peculiarity is its special relationship with, its special form of engagement with, language . . . a relationship which is intellectual and emotional at the same time and, more, is almost always a relationship by values. Ruskin said, 'Tell me what you like and I'll tell you what you are.' We could just as easily say, 'Tell me what language you use and I will tell you what you are.' Language is not simply a range of conventional signs, increasing and altering so as to express the world's complexity; the business of grappling with the world's complexity, with the life by time and the life by values, is itself partly carried on *through* and *within* language.

Literature can never be aesthetically 'pure' or abstractly contemplative. There can be no such thing as 'abstract literature' as there is such a thing as abstract painting. By its nature—because its medium, language, is used by almost everybody in all sorts of everyday situations; and because it tries both to *say* and to *be* —literature is an art which invites impurities.

We might call it the most creaturely of the arts. Perhaps this is also a source of its strength. No other art, no other way of exploring human experience, bodies out so wholly and many dimensionally 'the felt sense of life', makes us feel first of all that the experience must have been just like that, that desire and will and thought would indeed all have been caught up with those gestures, those smells, those sounds. It's not reality; it's a mirroring: but it mirrors more nearly than any other imaginative or intellectual activity the *whole* sense of an experience.

Literature is both in time and outside time. It is in time because it works best when it creates a sense of a certain time and place and of particular persons, when it works through (and re-creates) identifiable life and manners . . . Tom Jones hiding in a particular copse with Molly Seagrim, Marvell lying in a certain garden, Dimitri Karamazov in *that* prison cell, Tess baptizing her baby in *that* cottage bedroom.

It is outside time in two ways. First, in a sense we are all used to: that, if it is rooted in time and place and is imaginatively penetrating, it will go beyond particular time and place and speak about our common humanity, will become—as we used to say more readily—universal.

Literature goes beyond time in a more subtle sense. To say discursively, fully to paraphrase, all that an imaginatively successful scene in fiction or drama or a poem says, means and is— to do this would take an impossibly long time and would be futile. It is of the essence of the scene's or the poem's meaning that all its elements simultaneously co-exist, do their work at the same time . . . so that you feel them all at once as you would in heightened moments of life, if you were sufficiently sensitive. The resources of language and form then work together to produce the peculiarly literary achievement, full of simultaneous meaning . . . Yeats writing 'the salmon-falls, the mackerel-

crowded seas', Cordelia replying 'No cause, no cause', Mrs.
Bulstrode facing her maimed life with 'Look up, Nicholas'. One
could not, even at six-volume length, 'write out the meaning'
of any one of these; in separating the elements by space and
time you would destroy the meaning.

But to respond to these meanings is not necessarily an easy
matter. One hardly needs to say nowadays that it is not good
sense to expect a work of any depth to yield all its meanings on
a first reading by almost anyone in almost any mood. Literature
is 'for delight', it is true—delight in recognition, in exploration
and in ordering, in the sense of increased apprehension, of new
and unsuspected relationships, and in aesthetic achievement.
But beyond a fairly simple level (for example, rhythmic incan-
tation) we have to work more and attend better if we want the
best rewards . . . here as in any other activity.

It follows that a wide hospitality is good. Nor need it be the
enemy of good judgment. The fact that some people use their
claim to being hospitable as an excuse for refusing to make dis-
tinctions is another matter; catholicity is not promiscuity.
Almost every writer with imaginative ability (that is, with some
capacity, no matter how intermittent or partial, to explore
aspects of experience through language), almost every such
writer will have some insights to give (if only about the disorder of a person or a generation) if we read him disinterestedly,
with 'a willing suspension of disbelief'.

Such a man may in general, or in particular aspects, be immature or irresponsible; we may think his statements about or
his assumptions as to the nature of human life untrue or perverse. If we do feel any of these things we should say so, as
precisely and strongly as we think necessary. But we ought to be
clear what it is we are attacking. Otherwise we may wholly
dismiss a man of some imaginative ability, but whose outlook
we find antipathetic, and will claim that we are making a judgment on his literary powers; conversely, we may deceive ourselves into believing that we find imaginative insight in a writer
whose views chime in with our own but who is, in fact, without

literary-creative ability. If we do not 'entertain as a possibility' the outlook of a writer while we are reading him we shall not really know what his outlook is, and will subsequently attack or praise a caricature of it.

'To entertain as a possibility' may not be the best form of words but it is hard to produce a better. It does not mean 'to accept', because the process is more subtle than that. It means to exercise an intellectual and emotional openness and charity. It means to be able to see for a while how someone can have such an outlook and to know what it feels like to have it, what the world looks like from that angle. To do this is not to 'surrender'. All the time, though not necessarily consciously or self-consciously, we are testing that outlook against life as we think we know it ourselves. With certain writers we will be all the time in a sharp double state . . . of entertaining and rejecting at once; but even then there are likely to be some moments when light is thrown on an aspect of human experience, and some attitude which we had pushed out of the field of our experience will prove to have more power than we had been ready to think.

In my experience, this is likely to be true of all but two kinds of literary effort. It is not true of work which, though full of 'right instincts' and intelligent technicalities, shows no effective literary imagination. Think, for example, of many of the thematic novels about moral conflict published during the past twenty years. Worse, to me, is the bodilessly aesthetic production which tries to treat words and forms as ends in themselves. I believe that literature is certainly in one sense 'play'—grave and absorbed play; but these are pointless arabesques. They do not explore, and their patterns neither mean nor mirror. This is why I neither like nor value, for instance, much of Oscar Wilde.

I do not think a trivial outlook on life will produce great literature. It may produce odd incidental insights; but, overall, a shallow view of life will reveal itself as the product of a shallow penetration into human experience. But I agree also with R. P. Blackmur who noted that we could learn something from second- and third-rate work, so long as we supplied our own irony towards it. You salt it yourself.

The *effects* of literature cannot be simply described—the moral effects, that is. I do not think these effects are direct or our experience would be a simpler matter than it is (good readers might then be good people, and perhaps good writers better human beings even than their good readers). In speaking about the moral impact of art we are not talking about a more complicated form of those ethically improving tales for children, most of which are irrelevant to the way imaginative literature actually works. Obviously, we can learn morally even if evil appears to triumph. 'Moral impact' does not mean a direct ethical prompting but the effect of literature on the temper with which we face experience.

But first, and as we have seen, literature does all the time seek to embody and articulate something of the 'mass and majesty' of experience. Most of us as individuals (and most of our societies) are constantly tending to narrow our focus, to ignore embarrassing qualifications and complexities, to make much of the rest of the world and all that experience with which we are not comfortable—to make all this into a mere backcloth to the stage on which our egos act comfortably. Literature can help to bring us up short, to stop the moulds from setting firm. It habitually seeks to break the two-dimensional frame of fixed 'being' which we just as habitually try to put round others, to make us see them again as three-dimensional people in a constant state of 'becoming'. Literature can have no more than a formal use for utterly damned souls—or for saints.

It is all the time implicitly inviting us both to remain responsive and alert and to extend our humanity; we do not talk quite so glibly about 'all farm labourers' or even about 'all Russians' after we have read Hardy or Turgenev. It is implicitly inviting us to widen and deepen our knowledge of ourselves and of our relations with others, to realize that life is more this—and more that—than we had been willing to think (Emma at Box Hill, Queequeq looking down into the whale-nursery).

Lawrence's famous passage about the power of the novel ('It can inform and lead into new places the flow of our sympathetic consciousness . . .') is too well known to need quoting in full. George Eliot said much the same: 'If it does not enlarge men's sympathy, it does nothing morally', and spoke also about the need for 'truth of feeling . . . reverence . . . love . . . humaneness'.

All this, we have to remember, may be achieved—may sometimes only be achieved—in a mythic and parabolic way. When we speak of the 'moral intelligence of art' we are not speaking only of the will in action but also of a world outside the will, of the unconscious psychic life of men. It is important not to sound pretentious here; but literature—along with the other arts, which have their own ways of informing the imagination—can help us to rediscover awe.

What is true of individuals is true also of societies. A society without a literature has that much less chance of embodying within its temper and so within its organizations something of the fullness of human experience. We only know certain things by articulating them or by bodying them out. This does not mean that we have to 'argue them out'. We may know some things by approaching them metaphorically, as dramatic 'play'.

So literature can make us sense more adequately the fullness, the weight, the inter-relations and the demands of human experience—and the possibilities for order. It can make us feel all this, but not necessarily act on it. We can see and do otherwise, always. But we are not then acting quite so much out of blindness or inarticulateness; we are selfishly or fearfully or wilfully trying to short-cirucit what we know underneath to be more nearly the true state of things. Works of literature, properly read, give us the opportunity to extend our imaginative grasp of much in human experience; if we *will* to act well thereafter we may be able to do so with greater flexibility and insight. In this special sense literature can be morally educative. It can guide the moral will in so far as its illuminations depreciate certain modes of conduct and, conversely, reinforce others. But it cannot *direct* the moral will. In so far as it embodies moral intelligence and psychic insight it may *inform* the moral will, be 'the soul of all (our) moral being'.

So the relation of literature to 'the moral will' is not simple. Literature is 'a criticism of life' which must itself be judged. But we can only understand that criticism and make our own judgment on it if we first—in a sense—suspend the will, if we attend to the literature as itself, as if it were an autonomous created object, and let it work in its own way. It may then be in a close and active relationship with our sense of ourselves, inwardly and socially, with our sense of life in time and of life by values. Like the other arts, literature is involved with ends beyond itself. Things can never be quite the same again after we have read— really read—a good book.

RENÉ WELLEK

Some Principles of Criticism

————————————◆⊂◦⊃◆————————————

Literary criticism in the most widely accepted sense, is judgment of books, reviewing, and finally the definition of taste, of the tradition, of what is a classic. In our time T. S. Eliot has been the most influential taste-changer and taste-maker. But there is another concept of criticism which equates it with a scheme of principles, with poetics, with a theory of literature. This has been my own preoccupation, because it interests me and because, coming from the Continent to England and the United States, I felt strongly that there is a particular need of theoretical awareness, conceptual clarity and systematic methodology in the English-speaking countries, dominated as they are by the tradition of empiricism.

Theory of literature is not, of course, incompatible with an interest in individual works of art. On the contrary, we cannot arrive at principles, concepts or systems *in vacuo*: we must start with a study of the literary work itself. Minute analysis, 'close reading', is impossible without power of observation, without sensitivity to detail, and hence without interest, involvement, enjoyment. There is no contradiction between literary theory and experience, as the enemies of theory assume. As long ago as 1831, John Stuart Mill complained: 'he is a theorist: and the word which expresses the highest and noblest effort of human intelligence is turned into a byeword of derision'.

If we want to arrive at a coherent theory of literature, we must do what all other sciences do: isolate our object, establish our subject-matter, distinguish the study of literature from other neighbouring disciplines. It seems obvious that the work of literature is the central subject-matter of a theory of literature: not the biography or psychology of the author nor the social background nor the affective response of the reader. In *Theory of Literature*, published by Austin Warren and myself in 1949, I tried to draw a distinction between 'intrinsic' and 'extrinsic' methods in the study of literature and to emphasize the need of an intrinsic approach, i.e., an analysis of the work of art itself as a linguistic structure, as a system of meaningful signs. I thought (and still think) that the study of the extrinsic circumstances in which literature is set has far outgrown interest in the works themselves, that literary study has lost its centre, has become identical with the history of culture, with Carlyle's *Allerleiwissenschaft*.

This stress on the work itself, on its 'literariness', on the difference between art and life, has brought the charge of 'aestheticism', or 'formalism' or whatever disparaging noun can be found for anybody who holds fast to the insight of the great tradition of aesthetics descended from Kant. But recognition of the autonomy of art does not mean aestheticism in the sense in which it was understood at the end of the last century. 'Aestheticism' in that sense is pan-aestheticism, the illicit attempt to extend aesthetic criteria to ethics, politics, religion and metaphysics. On the contrary, I insist on distinguishing these realms, and I consider it a disservice to literature (and the other arts) to burden them with functions they cannot fulfil.

A work of art is not a social or historical document, not rhetorical exhortation, not religious revelation, not philosophical speculation—even though it can for certain purposes be viewed as such. Art is 'illusion', 'fiction', the world changed into language, paint or sound. It seems to me an oddity of our time that this simple insight into the aesthetic fact is construed as a denial of the relevance, the humanity and significance of art. The recognition of the difference between life and art, of the 'ontological gap' between a product of the mind, a linguistic structure, and the events in 'real' life which it reflects, does not and cannot mean that the work of art is a mere empty play of forms, cut off from reality. The relation of art to reality is not as simple as older naturalistic theories of copying or 'imitation' or Marxist 'mirroring' assume. 'Realism' is not the only method of art. It excludes three-quarters of the world's literature. It minimizes the role of imagination, personality 'making'.

If we grasp the central aesthetic fact, we shall then relegate to the periphery certain problems which have preoccupied many students of literature: biography, the psychology of the author, social conditions, and the like. But it is a misreading of this point of view to call it 'anti-cognitive', as George Watson does in *The Literary Critics* (Penguin, 1962, page 221), or even anti-historical. Obviously the emphasis on the work of art as a totality of meaning and value implies a distrust of the older factualism, the literary history preoccupied with anecdotes, sources and influences, the whole mosaic of information accumulated in the last two centuries. Antiquarianism has no doubt its place as an auxiliary for criticism, and it is enjoyed by its practitioners for its own sake. But erudition must not be confused with criticism.

Obviously, also, 'appreciation', sensitivity, the art of reading, is not enough. It does not and cannot lead to an organized body of knowledge, to theory. But, on the other hand, literary theory is not science in the sense of natural science, as humanists seem to fear. I am acutely aware of the difference between the humanities and the sciences, between criticism concerned with an interpretation of individuality and the modern scientific ideal of quantification and abstract laws. It seems decidedly odd that Wellek and Warren's *Theory of Literature* has been exhibited as an example of American scientism by an American writing in *Scrutiny*, of all places (Vol. XVI, September 1949). Obviously, an aesthetic point of view will also reject the interpretation of literature as 'mental therapy' offered by I. A. Richards, and it will revolt against the growing tendency of our time to mysticism and sheer obscurantism. The grandiose confusion of the now fashionable 'myth' criticism obliterates the distinction between myth and poetry, and the groping speculations of the existentialist critics use or misuse the work of literature as evidence for man's varying attitudes toward time and eternity.

The task of criticism will be a phenomenology of literature. It will be primarily concerned with an analysis of a literary work which will go beyond the usual impressionisms and the old dualism of content and form. 'Organism', while good enough as a term for the unity of content and form, is misleading for its biological parallelism, and does not get us very far. A conception of the work of art as a stratified structure is more helpful, at least as a beginning. It will work with linguistic and stylistic methods as long as we are concerned with the sound-stratum (euphony, metre, and the like) and the units of meaning (diction, syntax, style). But literary study cannot be reduced to sylistics (as we sometimes are told by such eminent practitioners of the art as Dámaso Alonso). Criticism must also go beyond language to the 'world' of the poet: the dusty slums and dreary provincial towns of Dostoevsky, haunted by possessed and ardent hearts; or to the far more elusive worlds of a Mallarmé or Rilke. These should not be confused with the real world.

The analysis of a work of art necessarily leads to an analysis of other works by the same author, other works written in the same genre, in the same period, in the same tradition. There is a simultaneous order of literature, and it is an order changing in history, as T. S. Eliot has stated memorably. *Theory of Literature* has been wrongly understood to advocate a purely static study of literature. It concludes rather with an emphatic last chapter on literary history, which pleads for a renewal of literary history, not as an illustration of social history or an account of a series of disconnected works chronologically arranged, but as an internal history of the art and tradition of literature. In several of my theoretical papers, recently collected as *Concepts of Criticism* (Yale University Press, 1963), I have tried to re-examine the main historiographical tools of the literary scholar: the concept of evolution, which seems to have disappeared from recent practice completely; the concept of period, which must neither be reduced to a linguistic label nor exalted to a metaphysical entity, but should be understood as the dominance of a system of literary conventions and norms whose rise and fall we can trace; and, finally, the specific period concepts which have given rise to such endless debates: Baroque, Romanticism, Realism.

Still, the concern for a literary history as art history—something taken for granted by historians of art or music—must not be understood as a rejection of the social and historical interpretation of literature. I am simply sceptical of the facile determinism prevalent in the studies of sources and influences whether social or literary. All determinism, all causal explanation seems to fail in the study of literature. It is never successful in establishing what one would consider the first requirement of any causal relationship: 'When X occurs, Y must occur.' I am not aware that any literary historian has ever given proof of such a necessary relationship. The reduction of a work of art to its causes is impossible because works of art are wholes, conceived in the free imagination, whose integrity and meaning are violated if we break them into sources and influences.

The critical analysis of a work of art, of its metre or rhythm, its diction and style, its metaphors and symbols, its characters, events and settings, must not be conceived as a purely 'objective' neutral process divorced from value judgment. Nothing, in literature, is a neutral fact, there is no feature which has not been selected by an act of critical judgment, and there is no detail in a work of art which can be analysed by purely descriptive means. The detail always functions in a whole whose very nature is value. It is a mistake to think that values are imposed on a work of art. The work of art is a structure of value, and the value has to be discerned by the critic. All attempts either to drain value away from literary study or to make it a science on the analogy of botany must fail.

Analysis, interpretation, evaluation are interconnected stages of a single procedure. Evaluation grows out of understanding. Correct evaluation out of correct understanding. What is correct interpretation of a specific work of art will, of course, be often a matter of dispute, but it seems impossible to deny that there is this problem of 'correctness' or 'adequacy' of interpretation, of a hierarchy of viewpoints. We might argue about the different concepts of Hamlet propounded by Goethe, Coleridge, A. C. Bradley, Ernest Jones, L. L. Schücking, Dover Wilson, and so on, but we must recognize that there are limits set to the freedom of interpretation: Hamlet is not a woman in disguise, nor is he, as Miss Winstanley proposed, 'mainly James I'. Just as there is correct interpretation, at least as an ideal, so there is correct judgment, good judgment.

Thus, we ought not to succumb to the lure of 'historicism' which spread from Germany and nowadays is still the almost official creed of many eminent scholars. 'Historicism' of this kind is only relativism and scepticism, an abdication before the task of criticism as judgment. The view that we must judge merely by the criteria of the past, that there is an unending multiplicity of irreconcilable standards—not only the poetry of Pope and the poetry of Wordsworth, but every poet's distinct and unique value—would, if carried through consistently, lead to an end of all literary appreciation, to complete anarchy, to the victory of the old vicious maxim, *De gustibus non est disputandum.*

Actually, there is wide agreement on the major authors, on the canon of literature, on the difference between great and thoroughly bad art. The whirligig of taste moves quickly only with secondary authors. There is an abyss in quality between Tolstoy and Ian Fleming, Dante and Grace Metalious. The relativist's argument from the tremendous variety of art holds good only against the narrow dogmatism, the frozen Absolute of an older classicism. Because we enjoy and understand Homer and T. S. Eliot, Grimms' *Fairy Tales* and Joyce, we can recognize that there is something common to all literature and all art: the aesthetic quality which is inadequately described by the traditional term 'Beauty'.

The world-wide spread of literature, its essential humanity, the close interconnexions of works of art, the survival of traditions and themes over gulfs of time and space are convincing arguments against the provincial and nationalistic limitations of most critics and literary historians in many lands. Neither English literature nor any other literature can be studied in isolation. Thus 'comparative literature' (a study not academically recognized in Great Britain, though expanding in the United States) seems to me an imperative need for a healthy development of literary studies, even though I have argued insistently against the narrow conception of Comparative Literature prevalent particularly in France. It must not be an arid, academic exercise in the study of external influences, reputations, migrations of themes and the like, but an investigation of the unity of literature, especially Western literature: of its great currents, periods and movements. 'Comparative Literature' is possibly an unfortunate term. Ideally, we should simply study literature without linguistic restrictions: consider all literature our province; have Professors of Literature, rather than English, French or German literature, as we still have Professors of Philosophy and History. Ideally, the Orient should be included in our purview, and comparative poetics should draw on literatures which have arisen without contacts with the West.

I myself come from a small nation at the crossroads of Europe, Czechoslovakia, and thus I feel that I can look at the great literatures with some detachment. The fate of emigration to the United States has only strengthened my sense of seeing Europe as a whole, from the other shore. But I have kept my interests in Czech literature, as witness my recent collection of *Essays on Czech Literature* (Mouton, The Hague, 1963), and no less my love for English literature, the field of my early specialization. As a young man I was carried away by English poetry, by Shakespeare, by Donne, by Marvell, on whom I wanted to write a monograph, by Pope, by the great Romantic poets, by Yeats and Eliot. This was the main attraction which brought me to England, to the Reading Room of the British Museum, when I was barely twenty-one.

My literary knowledge has since expanded widely: my tastes

have changed and shifted, reverted to early loves and discovered new beauty far afield. In recent years I have devoted much of my energy to writing a large-scale *History of Modern Criticism*, in which I plan to bring the story from the middle of the eighteenth century down to our day. Two volumes were published in 1955 (Yale University Press and Jonathan Cape); two more are to come, *deo volente*. The *History* tries to live up to my critical principles: it will include all the main western countries, Russia and Czechoslovakia not excepted. It is concerned with tracing the history of literary theory, and thus tries to steer a middle course between general aesthetics on the one hand and mere literary opinion on the other.

But I am convinced that literary theory cannot be divorced either from general aesthetics, on the one hand, or, on the other, from practical criticism in the sense of judgment and analysis of single works of art. I thus did not and could not write the kind of book that Saintsbury provided when he deliberately rejected all interest in theory and aesthetics. My *History of Modern Criticism* is conceived as a support and justification of the theory of literature. Theory is to emerge from history, just as history itself, in its turn, can be understood only with a system of questions and answers in mind. Neither historical relativism nor an unhistorical doctrinaire absolutism is the answer, but a 'perspectivism' which tries to see the object from all possible sides. Such a perspectivism assumes that there is an object: the elephant in spite of all the diverse opinions of the blind men. How can the opinion be justified that the literary critic is not merely another blind man, seizing the trunk, the tusk, the tail or the foot of the elephant alone? The only answer is precisely history and the lesson which grows out of it: a body of doctrines and insights, judgments and theories which are the accumulated wisdom of mankind. History and theory explain and implicate each other; there is a profound unity of fact and idea, past and present.

W. W. ROBSON

Are Purely Literary Values Enough?

————————————————

Two passages from T. S. Eliot's criticism have stuck in my mind for many years, and I will use them as a starting-point. In a lecture called 'Religion and Literature', published in 1936, Eliot writes:

'The "greatness" of literature cannot be determined solely by literary standards; though we must remember that whether it is literature or not can be determined only by literary standards.'

And in some lectures on 'Johnson as Critic and Poet', given in 1944, he observes that:

'In our own day the influence of psychology and sociology upon literary criticism has been very noticeable. On the one hand, these influences of social disciplines have enlarged the field of the critic, and have affirmed, in a world which otherwise is inclined to depreciate the importance of literature, the relations of literature to life. But from another point of view this enrichment has also been an impoverishment, for the purely literary values, the appreciation of good writing for its own sake, have become submerged when literature is judged in the light of other considerations.'

These two passages are not, of course, making the same point; but they seem to carry the same implication: that there exist 'purely literary values', and 'literary standards', which are relevant to 'the appreciation of good writing for its own sake'. In one case it is said that these standards are not sufficient to decide whether or not a work can be called great; in the other, that they can be distinguished from the kinds of criteria applied by critics who bring to bear a psychological or sociological interest in literature. We are not told, in either context, what they positively *are*: Eliot seems to assume that we already know, and merely need reminding. But in the context of the second quotation he does indicate what in his view they are *not*, by referring to the connexion of criticism, in the case of Coleridge, with 'philosophy and a theory of aesthetics'; in the case of Arnold, with 'ethics and propaedeutics'; and with an aberration unspecified in the case of Pater, but which we might guess to be the use of ostensibly critical writing for the purpose of quasi-creative 'self-expression'. Presumably, then, the implied contrast is with Dr. Johnson's approach to literature (Johnson being the subject of the lectures); and this reminder is felt to be enough to give substance to the phrases 'literary standards' and 'purely literary values'.

Eliot seems to be thinking of Johnson's practice, when discussing poetry, of detailed technical fault-finding. But is it not odd to lay stress on *this* as exceptionally characteristic and distinctive of Johnson's approach to literature; to insist that *this* above all is the lesson we are to learn from it? Any really central account would be bound to bring out how much Johnson was concerned, precisely, with 'the relations of literature to life'; and surely Johnson as little as any of the classical critics would have been inclined to regard problems about the greatness of literature as somehow extra-literary. Need one quote his remark about *Paradise Lost* that 'the want of human interest is always felt', or his famous paragraph on 'the praise of Shakespeare'?

But I have questioned the term 'purely literary values' not in order to deny that there are such things but to urge that our conception of them should not be too exclusive. Clearly the domain of the 'purely literary' *could* be very constricted. One might regard it as limited, for example, to the preservation (at any rate in discursive prose) of conventional grammar and syntax—or spelling. Or—advancing a little farther—one could

D   49

refer it to the kind of considerations dealt with in Fowler's *Modern English Usage*. Or one might think of the corrective procedures used in Graves's and Hodge's entertaining manual *The Reader over Your Shoulder*. But even here larger questions are likely to intrude; for how can we castigate, and try to rewrite, a supposedly faulty original without risking possibly quite serious judgments on the author's quality of mind, on his subject and his attitude towards it, on the purpose of his writing, and the extent to which it succeeds or fails? Stylistics may be an acknowledged field of study; but as soon as considerations about *value* enter it—and questions of relative success or failure cannot but involve them—its practitioner is committed to doing literary criticism in the usual sense, whether that is what he calls it or not. And we may note that Eliot speaks of literary *standards* as determining at least *some* questions of literary value.

To insist on the retention of 'literary standards' and 'purely literary values' ought merely to mean that criticism should be relevant. But this does not settle anything, for it leaves open the question, what are the canons of relevance. It seems plain that to frame these narrowly is undesirable. But more than that, it is quite unplausible. To take an analogy: there might well be a 'purely musical' analysis of Elgar's *Falstaff* which entirely ignored the fact that the music was intended, among other things, to recall the character and career of Falstaff. But it seems to me that there is simply *no equivalent* 'purely literary' analysis of Shakespeare's *Henry IV*. Twentieth-century critics of Shakespeare may be wary of talking about characters; Falstaff has even been called 'a walking symbol', or 'a triumphant particular crystallization' of some general element in the poetic drama. But the authors of these phrases would no doubt grant it to be of the first importance that whatever was symbolized or crystallized did not take the form of a *thin* man. In fact, of course, the whole of Shakespeare's Falstaff ought ideally to be present in the consciousness of the critic of *Henry IV*, as he need not be in the critic of Elgar's music.

'Purely literary values' may be found an objectionable expression by those who associate it with the discredited doctrine of aestheticism. What exactly this doctrine is (in relation to literature) I do not know. It does not seem to be stated clearly anywhere. To me, it suggests not a doctrine but a tendency or attitude, though one now perhaps existing chiefly in the imaginations of philosophers whose paradigm-situation for the experience of art seems to be a man gazing at a Chinese vase. How *his* postulated 'pure aesthetic experience' can intelligibly be compared with anything we are supposed to do with *Middlemarch* or the *Bacchae* or *The Death of Ivan Ilyich*, I do not know. Certainly I cannot believe that our ideal experience of these or any other great works of literature can be regarded as some sort of pure intuition of formal beauty unrelated to the human substance and significance of the works, irrelevant to our sense of human needs and purposes, or excluding (on the ground that a great work of art is unique and *sui generis*) our sense of comparative value in other literature and in life.

None the less, I think there is something to be learnt from the common tendency of aestheticians to assimilate literature to the 'purer' arts. And that is an emphasis on the *contemplative* element in our experience; or, to put it another way, on our sense that what we are experiencing is *art*, that of its nature it is not arbitrary or gratuitous, but made by a human being for certain purposes, in a certain mode, convention, or 'frame'. Our sense of what this 'frame' is may vary widely in different cases. Sometimes it is as if the writer actually asks us to include our awareness of the convention he is using as an important part of what he offers us; as perhaps in Marvell's Nymph complaining of the death of her fawn. At the other extreme, as in some of D. H. Lawrence's poetry, the writer seems to be doing all he can to make us forget the 'frame', and to participate directly not only in the experience offered by the completed poem but also in the experience that prompted it. And there are all sorts of other cases, more or less complex; Coleridge's famous 'suspension of disbelief', originally formulated with reference to dramatic illusion, is merely one refinement of the make-believe which

51

comes naturally in the nursery, and which in the experience of art may take much more sophisticated forms. But all these modes of experience entail not necessarily a continuity of critical consciousness of what we are doing and of what is being done to us but at least the capacity to return at any moment to such consciousness. We may be imaginary participants in what is going on, but we can always resume the role of spectator. As a rule, perhaps, we seem to be both spectator and participant at once; and this is as near as I can get to suggesting the characteristic stance, or attitude, or frame of mind, in which we appreciate important art. Naturally the degree of involvement will depend not merely on the kind of work in question but on the recipient. I have the impression that in his experience of art the distinguished critic George Santayana was almost wholly a spectator, and that in his case we would not speak of a possible *reversion* to the contemplative mode, since he never left it. But this sort of detachment is rare. The essential experience of art is surely a more full-blooded and full-bodied response than the word 'contemplation' suggests. And yet I suggest that no art is worthy of the name if it cannot survive this kind of attention to how it does what it does.

But I do not wish to dwell on the subtler aspects of the literary experience, in case I should be thought to be implying that the qualities of a work which are relevant to criticism are in any way recondite. Indeed, the real difficulty is to know what to *exclude*; to commit oneself to saying what is not, or never, relevant. Certain considerations—say, biographical ones—can sometimes be ruled out as external, as not manifestly 'in the work'. But this familiar prescription can be harder to apply than it looks. Is Henry Fielding's personal character relevant to the appreciation of his writings? I should say, decidedly yes. True, we need not go outside *Tom Jones* to infer it. We can point to the warm, compassionate, masculine strength so evident in Fielding's best work. But it would be critical purism to maintain that our sense of this is not increased by our knowledge of the biographical facts; or that we ought, as critics, to try to keep this knowledge out of our minds. What we make of a work depends on what we bring to it; and justice and fairness in literary matters do not require that we approach literature with a blank mind, if indeed that is possible. Literature is a fully human product, and a sense of the author as whole may be indispensable to our pleasure and our understanding. Certainly we need a sense of proportion, and some degree of critical—not to say ethical—conscience; but these need not be developed very far, in a reader whose interest is in poetry not gossip, before he can decide (for example) just how much of *Dylan Thomas in America* is relevant, or irrelevant, in making up his mind about Dylan Thomas's poems.

The objection to the hypothetical aesthete, or the critical purist, is the same essentially as the objection to those who censor literature in the interests of a conventional morality. In both cases too much that we know to be vitally important to literature, as literature, is being handed over to an external judgment. I certainly do not deny that literature reflects, or contains, or—perhaps it is best to say—embodies moral values. But it seems to me that these are merely certain of its characteristic values looked at in a certain way. Among all the curiously varied travesties that Dr. Leavis has been the victim of in his long career, the one that comes nearest to being recognizable is the label of 'rugged moralist'. This, of course, is applied sarcastically, with the implication that he tends to introduce non-literary factors into his criticism—the didactic, or the puritanical. But surely when we disagree with his more comprehensive judgments on literature, it is not because he has gratuitously introduced a 'moral' note at a point where it is unexpected, or inappropriate, but either because one does not agree with the moral views implicit in those judgments, or (as in my own case) because the work in question either does or does not seem to embody the moral values that he finds, or misses, there. To take a minor example that comes to mind: how much of Lawrence's customary respect for life can be found in his attitude towards Mr. Massy, the 'little abortion' in *The Daughters of the Vicar*?

But even when such disagreements are more serious and far-reaching, does one really find that what Leavis's opponents are objecting to is some moralistic irrelevance? Or are they objecting to the introduction of moral questions at all? Surely the case is rather that the opponents have—or think they have—different moral views.

A point should be made here about terminology. It is an unfortunate by-product of the controversy about aestheticism (one going back to the last century) that the word 'moral' tends to be used to cover everything humanly important, meaningful and serious in the imaginative literature that we read with full attention. And the wide and vague application of the word deprives it of its value as a means of indicating a certain stress and focus in the preoccupation demanded of the reader. But despite all its possibly misleading suggestions, it can never be abandoned. It reminds us of a dimension of life from which we can never escape if we are to remain human. And the moral element in literature is unevadable on literary grounds, at any rate for the writer who is committed in any way ('realist', 'naturalist', or other) to fulfilling the standard of 'truth to life'. What truth to life can there be in his work, if it ignores the moral experience of mankind? It is simply a fact that human beings *are* moral, and attempts to evade this fact in the interests of 'realism' are as unrealistic as any romance. True, a writer may take up (or believe that he is taking up) a consistent attitude of moral detachment from the characters, *mores*, and conduct he is depicting. But once again literary considerations, considerations of art, make it difficult to suppose that a work composed in this spirit could be of any interest. It would require some pretence on the writer's part of being 'above' or 'below' the human level, which (again appealing to the realistic canon he has accepted) must inevitably falsify his rendering; we cannot see human life from the point of view of a fly, or of the deities of Lucretius. Of course, no successful or interesting work has ever been really composed in this spirit; if Flaubert thought he had done so, he was mistaken.

The question, then, whether moral judgments are relevant in literary criticism seems to me an unreal one, unless we are given a clear statement of the moralist's (or anti-moralist's) notion of the characteristically literary judgments with which the moral judgments are alleged to be contrasted. To take a familiar example: when we say, as most people do, that the business of Little Nell in *The Old Curiosity Shop* is mawkish, is that a 'moral judgment'? It certainly bears not only on the question of Dickens's application of his intelligence in this part of his work but also (if these can be separated) on the degree of his self-knowledge and his respect for his art and for his readers. And yet this judgment is surely *typical* of the sort of thing we expect to be asserted or denied about a work like this; it seems no more extra-literary than the judgment 'People don't behave like that', which everyone would agree to be relevant to the appraisal of realistic fiction. To say that Little Nell is mawkish is simply to say that Little Nell is bad art.

Someone might say that this kind of concern is more likely to come up when novels and the like are before us. The scope and subject-matter of a *War and Peace* invite more portentous and far-reaching decisions than, for instance, a short lyric. But I do not think it is true that the essential criteria in the two cases are different in logical type. Obviously considerations of mode, weight, and substance must play their part in any intelligent discussion; but we have only to reflect on the criteria according to which we might express a preference, say, for Wordsworth's 'A slumber did my spirit seal' over Housman's 'The night is freezing fast' to find that we are still appealing in the end to the same vital principles, at the same depth.

Anyone who has taken part in teaching literature to grown-up people, or in the public discussion of it, will have encountered the dogged and naive questioner whose primary requirement of literature is the 'sincerity' of the author. This student is nowadays the object of sophisticated mockery from modern-minded academics and literary reviewers. I believe that he is right; and my object in writing is to provide him with adequate intellectual

defence against this derision. Clearly the term 'sincerity' is open
to misuse. Being a psychological term, it can distract our attention from the only relevant object of literary criticism—the
work itself—to dubiously pertinent and anyway difficult questions about the hypothetical state of mind of the author at the
time of composition, or his motives for writing. And it has the
further drawback that it seems only obviously applicable to those
works (poems, say) in which the author speaks or appears to
speak in his own person. And even 'personal' poems are not
affidavits. Sincerity is easily confused with autobiography, and
inquiries about where the author's materials came from. Nothing
has done Sir Philip Sidney's reputation as a poet more unjust
harm than the discovery that (having told us how on his Muse's
instructions he looked in his heart and wrote) he looked into the
work of Italian poets. Then, sincerity cannot be a *sufficient* condition of excellence, as many a hymn, epitaph, or undergraduate
love poem will show. At most, it can only be a necessary condition; and as such may not be thought to tell us much.

For all these reasons I have sometimes thought that the word
might be replaced by some such term as 'genuineness' or
'authenticity', which do at least point to the created object and
not to the soul of its creator. But I have now come to believe
that, like the term 'moral', 'sincerity' cannot be abandoned. It
implies, or should imply, a profound personal self-commitment
of the writer. But this commitment is very different from that of
'committed' (or propaganda) literature, which cannot of its very
nature reflect the inward and intimate movements of the human
will. The relevant kind of sincerity is something that has to be
achieved by an inner discipline. Our sense of it is a sense that the
writer has himself lived through in imagination what his work
affirms or rejects, expresses or fails to express, reveals or leaves
in shadow; its doubts, its tensions, its final moral poise. I do not
mean that a work need be, in our actual experience of it,
obviously an imaginative living-through of the writer's own
problems, in a way in which this quotation from *Jude the Obscure*
may suggest:

'As you got older, and felt yourself to be at the centre of your time, and not at a point in its circumference, as you had felt when you were little, you were seized with a sort of shuddering. . . . All around you there seemed to be something glaring, garish, rattling and the noises and glares hit upon the little cell called your life, and shook it, and warped it'

Jude the Obscure itself looks in part like such a work, and one reason for its unsatisfactoriness is that we are not sure quite how far it *is* that, and how far it is an objective case-history with a sociological 'moral'; we have doubts as to whether Hardy altogether knows what he is doing. But that this process of imaginative living-through has *preceded* the work, and underlies what has become dramatic creation, we have a right to be assured; and our assurance comes not from external sources but from our own reading, when we do it with the full force of our minds. Our feeling about this profound and absolute sincerity of the author is an essential part of our recognition of his full humanity.

This full humanity in great writers can be the reverse of reassuring. It can even be frightening. Let us professional teachers and aspirant critics of literature ask ourselves how much of our theoretical system-building, and conviction about our taste, springs from fear—fear of the greatness of literature, fear of ourselves or of our pupils, fear of sincerity whether in ourselves or in others. I do not wish to impute motives to anyone else; as George Herbert says, 'My God, I mean myself'. But I cannot help wondering if there is not something generally amiss about the frequent academic insistence on the historical approach, or on the importance of genres. How pain-saving it can be to remind oneself and one's pupils that the humiliation of Malvolio was arranged for an Elizabethan audience which enjoyed bearbaiting; or that in order to get *The Merchant of Venice* right we should adopt in imagination what seems a very quaint and medieval attitude towards Jews (as I think we in fact have to do if we are fully to enjoy Chaucer's *Prioress's Tale*). How convenient it is to disallow any sympathy with the poor old carpenter of the Miller's Tale, on the ground that this after all is 'farce', without noting how the impulsion towards sympathy, inhibited in the tale itself by the farcical atmosphere, is given its rights in the reaction of the old Reeve who objects to it, with his monologue that is at once comic and pathetic and something else.

But these are not seriously testing cases. The most difficult test for me, as to whether I can accept the full humanity of great literature, is that dark note of misanthropy, which sometimes is to be heard there. One can perhaps 'place' the misanthropy of a Swift, as part of the case of a radically distorted genius. But what about the misanthropy to be found in Shakespeare, in Tolstoy, in D. H. Lawrence? All I can say is that we must be very sure of just what are our motives for rejecting it; if they arise purely from the instinctive movement of health; or if it is rather that we are not facing something in ourselves, something perhaps giving rise to, and concealed by, our desire to seem to ourselves and to others always 'nice', placatory, and well-adjusted social beings.

The real reading and teaching and discussion of literature are bound to be processes of self-testing and self-exposure; we have to find out, and be prepared to reveal, and to commit ourselves sturdily to, what we think funny, or cruel, or wise, or compassionate, or silly, or boring, or good. Perhaps what we shall eventually discover—the thing that matters most of all, finally, in our dealings with great literature—is what is our conception of *nobility*, of the noble life: or if we have one. We should not be afraid of this word because of its associations with outdated Victorian solemnity. I do not like—it seems to me revealing, in a tiny way, of something unwholesome in our society—the present fashion of casual sneering at one of the greatest Victorian writers, George Eliot. How much of English literature—how much of Russian—do the people who do this really have access to?

But I am not suggesting that we can take over (how could we?) any previous writer's conception of the noble. We have to work out our own; but since this is difficult to do, it is natural that we should turn more and more to the writers whom we recognize as classics. I have no wish to indulge in any topical jeremiads; but the obvious decline of, or—to put it less tendentiously—the obvious uncertainty about standards of honour, conduct and manners, to be seen in current fiction no less than in the newspapers and the life around us, makes it all the more important that we should get all the help we can from the past towards understanding ourselves and our problems. After reading Chapter LXXIV of *Middlemarch*, we might ask ourselves if there is alive and active in the literature of our own day the kind of compassionate intelligence that informs this treatment of human degradation and pain:

'It was eight o'clock in the evening before the door opened and his wife entered. He dared not look up at her. He sat with his eyes bent down, and as she went towards him she thought he looked smaller—he seemed so withered and shrunken. A movement of new compassion and old tenderness went through her like a great wave, and putting one hand on his which rested on the arm of the chair, and the other on his shoulder, she said, solemnly but kindly—

'"Look up, Nicholas."

'He raised his eyes with a little start and looked at her half amazed for a moment: her pale face, her changed, mourning dress, the trembling about her mouth, all said "I know"; and her hands and eyes rested gently upon him. He burst out crying and they cried together, she sitting at his side. They could not yet speak to each other of the shame which she was bearing with him, or of the acts which had brought it down on them. His confession was silent, and her promise of faithfulness was silent. Open-minded as she was, she nevertheless shrank from the word which would have expressed their mutual consciousness as she would have shrunk from flakes of fire. She could not say "How much is only slander and false suspicion?" and he did not say "I am innocent".'

JOHN WAIN

Notes on Imagination and Judgment

————————◆⊃◦⊂◆————————

'The human mind is so made that it is capable of growth, and of growth in part through its own self-directed effort.'

YVOR WINTERS

Literature exists in order to tell the truth. As a preliminary statement this is essential, but it will not be much use to us unless we go on to ask, 'What kind of truth? The truth about what?'

Journalism is measured by its truthfulness to objective fact: and it is an accepted convention of our civilization that most journalism is slanted—it gives the facts that seem most attractive to the men who finance it—and is therefore not often completely truthful. Advertising, which uses the techniques of journalism to the specific end of selling certain products, is not even expected to be truthful in this sense; it is required by law not to tell outright lies, and there the matter ends. Literature, however—and by common consent we use the rather cumbrous term 'literature' to mean writing that has permanence and value —literature is the truth; that is what makes it literature. If a writer is telling lies about his material, if he is sentimentalizing or flattering or impoverishing what he knows about human life, he is automatically ruling himself out of court; what he writes may be profitable, it may be amusing and beguiling, but it is not 'literature'.

Having said this, we have begun. But we have done no more than begin. 'The truest poetry is the most feigning.' That paradox has been argued about, chewed over, pushed and pulled this way and that, ever since imaginative literature emerged as a separate human activity. The problem has always been to decide what kind of truth we are demanding from our writers. Until we know that, it is difficult to find a basis for praise or blame. For literature is not science. Science tells us about the physical world; literature, like the other arts, tells us what mankind has made of life in that world. If it is 'realistic', it tells us what the writer believes to be the objective truth about the *milieu* he finds himself living in. Since the outward look modifies the object, there is of course no such 'objective' truth. A housing estate on the outskirts of Sheffield might appear hell to a Chelsea artist, heaven to a Chinese coolie, and tolerable enough—'middle-earth'—to the people who actually live there. Each point of view is valid from its own position. Each is 'the truth'.

If, on the other hand, literature is not realistic but imaginative or even fantastic, it aims to tell us the truth about the dreams and aspirations of humanity rather than its objective circumstances. We learn from it what human beings want rather than what they have, or think they have. Sometimes, for instance, the race finds it necessary to live a whole epoch over again, imaginatively, in order to get full imaginative value from it. Thus the Middle Ages existed twice over: once as an actual period of time, stretching from about the twelfth century to the fifteenth, and once as an imaginative experience. Its second life began in the mid-eighteenth century and is just about coming to an end now. From Bishop Percy's *Reliques of Ancient English Poetry*, through Chatterton and Walpole to Scott, and then downwards from that peak to Chesterbelloc and Hollywood—it is the complete biography of an epoch's second existence.

Of course the idea of the Middle Ages projected during this second incarnation was, for the most part, illusory and totally false to the actual qualities of life in that epoch. But it would be foolish to censure this falsity too high-mindedly, even where it showed traces of definite dishonesty. Bishop Percy, for instance, knew that the ballads he published in his *Reliques* were not exactly true to the versions to be found in old manuscripts or collected among the peasantry. He touched them up because he loved them for certain qualities, and wanted these qualities to come out more strongly. The Middle Ages were not medieval enough for him, the romances insufficiently romantic. But in failing to give his readers the precise objective truth about the medieval poetic mind, he gave them something very true to the spirit of eighteenth-century romanticism. So that his anthology took its place with 'literature' rather than with scholarship. In our day these two partners are estranged; in his they shared a domicile.

Eighteenth-century medievalizing conveys an imaginative vision for which the men of that time felt a deep need. Trapped in the Age of Reason, with nothing ahead of them but the dust-bowl of industrialism and the guilty adventure of imperialism, they found, or claimed to have found, qualities in the civilization of their remote forefathers on which their minds delighted to dwell. In fact, the whole of eighteenth-century literature bears traces of this search for a way out. (I do not call it 'escapism' because 'escapism' is a very silly and very ugly word.) The account of the South Sea Islanders in a book like *Hawkesworth's Voyages*, for instance, is highly sentimentalized, and Hawkesworth knew exactly how sentimentalized it was, since he was working from the dry and objective accounts given by Cook, Banks and Solanger. (Cook's own account was not thought worth publishing till 1893, and then the editor was not a literary man but a naval officer.) But *Hawkesworth's Voyages*, day-dreaming though it is, contains the truth; not about the South Seas, but about England. To know a man's character you must know his compensatory fantasies as well as his responsible actions.

'But what about standards? If irresponsible fantasies are "true", and literature is equally hospitable to every kind of truth, does it not follow that any book is as good as any other?' The question has been building up ever since I began to outline my position, and must be answered before we can go any farther. The answer, unfortunately, is a cumbrous one. If I could resolve all difficulties in a few clear-cut sentences I would do it, in which case literary studies, especially as a medium of higher education, would lose most of their interest. For the fact is that it is just this problem that makes literary criticism a moral activity: and not only moral, but imaginative.

When we think of our own compensatory fantasies we can see clearly enough which of them are merely idle, vicious or irresponsible, and ought to be curbed, and which of them genuinely represent values which we try, or ought to try, to implement in our active lives. This kind of sorting-out is an important part of the moral life of the individual; and the critic who attempts it in the public field of literature is merely transferring the same activity to the mind of the race instead of his own mind. The same qualities are needed: a sense of reality, a delicacy, a generosity, and above all a genuine liking for the human animal. The puritanical self-disgust which shrinks from knowledge of its own sweat and dung, and then turns that revulsion outwards in a series of attacks on other people, is fatal to the literary sensibility just as it is fatal to the moral sensibility—indeed, just *because* it is so. The Pecksniff school of criticism, always witch-hunting for 'maturity' and denouncing as vicious and irresponsible any writing it happens not to like, will burn itself out in a few years; it cannot last, because the whole nature of literature is against it.

This is the central problem of criticism, the reason why it is a difficult art. We necessarily apply moral standards to literature, yet we are lost if we allow ourselves to apply those standards in a way that contradicts our human experience. Some of the most valuable critics have worked themselves round to a position in which they are asking for a literature that ignores truth. Even Samuel Johnson, whom I regard as the greatest English literary critic, lapsed for a moment into sadly muddled thinking when debating the propriety or otherwise of Cordelia's death in *King Lear*:

'A play in which the wicked prosper and the virtuous miscarry may doubtless be good, because it is a just representation of the common events of human life; but since all reasonable beings naturally love justice, I cannot easily be persuaded that the observation of justice makes a play worse; or that, if other excellencies are equal, the audience will not always rise better pleased from the final triumph of persecuted virtue.'

Even the language is slightly muddled; a 'just representation' is all very well in its way, but we would rather see 'justice'. It is so exceptional for Johnson to go wrong in this way that we may suspect a very strong emotional deflection. The death of Cordelia was particularly distressing to him, and he felt an almost personal resentment on finding that Shakespeare had not taken over this detail from the source, but invented it to deepen the tragic gloom of his fifth act. In this, Johnson 'rejoiced to concur' with the common eighteenth-century playgoer, since Nahum Tate's version of *King Lear* was then, and for many years afterwards, in firm possession of the stage, and in that version Cordelia survives. 'All reasonable beings love justice', so it is reasonable to bring it into a play; if 'the common events of human life' are not reasonable, not sane, not merciful, so much the worse for them. It is a very understandable *cri de coeur* from a man whose emotions are strongly involved, and it helps us to sympathize with similar deflections of judgment when we find them elsewhere: when Marxist critics labour to show that Chekhov was a progressive social reformer whose attitude to the declining landowners was simply disapproving and satirical; when people from repressive homes, who have had to fight with all their strength for sexual freedom, clamour that any book describing the act of copulation is a masterpiece; when the suburban middle class, brought up between privet hedges, find beatific revelation in any book, play or film about factory workers.

All these people are using literature as a means of wish-fulfilment, just as Johnson wanted Cordelia's life to be spared, at the catastrophe of the most titanic tragedy in the language, because he could not bear the pain of her death—though it is characteristic of him that he frankly made the admission that life *was* like that: a frankness very rarely encountered among Marxists, or sex-propagandists, or worker-worshippers. They make the mistake Johnson did not make, of confusing their personal wishes with the objective nature of things. Where he was content to say that a happy ending would make the play more enjoyable for the audience, and that he was not easily persuaded that it would diminish the value of the fiction, they assert baldly that the kind of writing that satisfies their prior appetites *is* the truth. They are unwilling to open their minds to new kinds of experience. Instead of seeing literature as a wider human activity, they want it to be propaganda for the things they happen to be interested in. As critics they are failures, and when, as often happens, they are also writers, they are even greater failures, no matter how loud the applause of their own *chapelle*.

One needs a good balance, plus a surprising amount of ordinary human decency, to be a good writer. This is the humble reality behind such claims as Milton's, when he said that a man who hoped to write memorable poetry 'must be himself a true poem'. Most writers discover, at some stage in their lives, that the process of turning oneself into a better literary artist becomes inextricably blended with that of turning oneself into a better *man*. The first steps—learning the craft of putting words together, mastering elementary techniques of prose or verse, narrative or drama—can be taken by a mind enclosed in its own egotism. The later steps cannot. The writer finds that he has to break out of his own entrenched personality and realize what it is like to be someone else. And gradually he realizes that humanity is made up of these mysterious other people. If he finds them distasteful, frightening, contemptible, he will either cease to be a writer, or settle down at the detective-story level. (This level is inhabited by many who have never written a detective story, including some who call themselves poets.)

If, on the other hand, the writer discovers that he does, fundamentally, like other people and wish them well, he will then find himself appalled at the dreadful things that can happen to them. This is the bridge that separates the tragic writer from the satirist. And every mature writer has the tragic sense, even if he never writes a tragedy. To be concerned for humanity is to be shocked at the evil that frequently overtakes them, and at the same time to forgive them for generating so much of this evil in their own natures. The writer cannot withdraw this concern every time he makes some fresh discovery about human greed or stupidity.

Love is not love
Which alters when it alteration finds.

Having used the word 'love', I find myself on a rhetorical peak with nowhere further to go. Painters love colours and shapes, musicians love sounds; writers, who use the instrument of language shaped for them by innumerable human mouths, and who deal in the adventures and misadventures of mankind, have to love people. And the only really bad writing is the kind that shows no trace of this love. Pornography, for instance, is not a serious evil because one can love humanity while admitting that it is often lustful. The current vogue for the exploitation of violence, on the other hand, is wicked because it takes pleasure in spotlighting the most negative of all human traits. If lust disappeared from the human consciousness, the race would be extinct in a few years. If violence and cruelty disappeared—i.e., were channelled into harmless activities such as games—who would be the worse? If I see a gang of youths coming towards me on a dark night, I am not particularly disturbed at the thought that they may have been reading books, or seeing films, which inflamed their desire for the opposite sex; but tell me they have been reading about James Bond or Mike Hammer, and I shall take to my heels. (To forestall an obvious objection, let me say that I should feel exactly the same if I were a woman, since rape is a form of violence more than a form of sexual indulgence.) Such writing shows a basic contempt for humanity, exploiting its self-destructive impulses as one exploits a pig's greed by rattling his swill-bucket to call him into the sty. A true writer knows that humanity has these impulses, as a humane farmer knows that pigs are greedy; but he knows that other qualities exist as well. The poet who decided that Cordelia must die, knew also that Miranda must live.

HARRY LEVIN

Leech-gathering

It is probably a healthy thing to be questioned about one's
professional reasons for existence, and when one's questioner
co-exists in a comparable sphere of endeavour one can only
hope that the question itself will not turn out to be mutually
rhetorical. Academic it is bound to be in the present instance,
since the respondent happens to be a professor by calling and a
critic mainly by courtesy. This means that he has managed to
gain his living through certain activities which he is not ordin-
arily called upon to justify, by reading as much as he could, by
mulling it over, by discussing it orally with students and now
and then with other readers through print.

It has been so purely pleasurable an assignment that I sometimes feel guilty at being paid for doing so little else. Hence I
find myself extremely vulnerable to the sort of query that
Wordsworth repeatedly put to his old Leech Gatherer on that
lonely moor. Just exactly what is it that one does? And how is it
that one lives? 'What occupation do you there pursue?' I would
that I could answer by patient example, and show no less reso-
lution or independence than did Wordsworth's dogged inter-
locutor. But criticism is never in its nature a solitary pursuit, and
whether or not its gleanings are salutary must be considered a
moot point. Happily, the invitation calls for a credo rather than
a confession, and one is not necessarily expected to live up to
everything that one professes to believe.

Professes? To believe? There is where the trouble begins.
The classical periods were field-days for criticism precisely be-

cause they could afford to take such professions of faith for granted; though opinions might individually differ, everyone could appeal to a single accepted code. If Samuel Johnson could lay down the law so authoritatively, it was because his literary authority rested upon authoritarian attitudes toward religion and politics. The subsequent growth of science and democracy, by fostering the development of alternative attitudes, challenged the traditional notion of culture and thereby created the dilemma that so perplexed Matthew Arnold.

Latter-day critics have had to face it in one way or another. Those who continue to play a judicial role have maintained their jurisdiction by narrowing their view: by embracing a dogma and addressing the faithful. Neo-orthodoxy has proved itself capable of moving in diametrically opposite directions: of excommunicating D. H. Lawrence, with T. S. Eliot, or proscribing Boris Pasternak, with the editors of the *Literaturnaya Gazeta*. In fairness to Mr. Eliot it should be remarked that his dogmatizing, unlike the Soviet kind, presupposes the prevalence of heresy. Yet heresy—which I can merely equate with a liberal outlook—thrives upon the stalemate of such conflicting attempts to conceive the world as a smaller and simpler place than the course of experience has actually shown it to be. Its very largeness may indeed have instigated partial viewpoints, party lines, and *Partisan Reviews*. In any case, the application of dogmatic principles, theological or ideological, is more objective than the unprincipled dogmatism of coteries.

Objectivity, in matters involving human responses, may at best be an approximation; none the less it lies within the critic's power to aim at Arnold's goal of 'disinterestedness'—to do his best, in other words, to detach himself from preconceptions and prejudices. Hence a credo may be somewhat less germane to his efforts than, in Holofernes's phrase, a *haud credo*, an emphatic disclaimer of all beliefs except an infrangible belief in literature itself. It is not for nothing that the commonest meaning of 'to criticize' is to censure, to dispense blame more readily than praise. The uncomfortable privilege of expressing discontent with the *status quo*, the sceptical habit of seeing through and beyond the trivial immediacies of man's condition, may well be man's clearest way of distinguishing himself from the animals. It is to be noted that Jean-Paul Sartre and his fellow proponents of *la littérature engagée* have been more effectual in their critique of things-as-they-are than in their commitment to a succession of causes.

Literature itself, to be sure, would quickly cease to exist if it were not constantly taking sides and projecting values; and every value-judgment has its significance in reckoning the total impact of any given work. All the more reason why literary criticism should stand by in sympathetic detachment, and set its sights by an ultimate prospect of understanding, rather than compromise itself by unduly engaging in the fluctuating traffic of revaluation. Too many Olympian verdicts have been reversed; too many hot tips have grown cold; too many absolutes have, with the passage of time, revealed limitations.

These cautionary reflections leave me open to the charge of being a relativist. I am quite willing to accept the term, if I am allowed the right to choose my definition. Relativism, for the absolutist, is a wholly negative conception, implying the absence of standards. I should prefer to regard it as a concern for ever-changing standards, both in their variety and in their continuity, as well as, much more positively, a sense of universal inter-relatedness—a sense which, in so far as I possess it at all, I owe to Alfred North Whitehead. Now every intellectual discipline is devoted to the study of certain unique relationships, large and small. Literary criticism, understandably, has found it more attractive to dwell upon the smaller particularities. But in so far as it constitutes a mode of knowledge it must likewise deal with broad and basic points of connexion.

My own critical focus has centred on two or three of these points: first and primordially, on the relation between literature and life. Perhaps no complex variable has been subject to more drastic oversimplifications. On the one hand, Marxists, publicists, and censors have confounded the two categories. On the other hand, the adherents of art-for-art's sake have refused to recognize any linkage between them. Each of these extreme positions has its characteristic source of strength. The social critics have well understood how art could be a weapon, and how its emotional charge could affect and reflect men's lives. In their turn, the formalists have insisted that it is first and last art, and have quickened appreciation of it with their intensive scrutinies.

This is not so much a contradiction as it is a complementarity. Of course the critic's starting-point is literature, though in a larger sense he has already started with life. The works that he examines are verbal artifacts which give sensuous pleasure, and may incidentally communicate ideas, through the writer's mastery of their aesthetic medium. Consequently there can be no adequate substitute for informed stylistic explication or detailed structural analysis; yet all such interpretation would be barren if it did not lead toward a meeting of minds between writer and reader. My own realization of the interplay between form and function, as demonstrated *a fortiori* through the elaborate conventions of the Homeric epic, was one of the lessons I learnt from Milman Parry.

I have tried to generalize the problem under the concept of 'Literature as an Institution', a highly tentative formulation which seeks to reconcile the autonomy of artistic usages with the responsive counterclaims of society. More concretely, I have been studying that conscious tendency on the part of writers to imitate life—moreover, to criticize it—which is so very loosely known as realism, and possibly to pin it down with a little more precision by relating it to the rise and decline of middle-class culture. Its special paradox is the unremitting competition between fact and fiction, which has *Don Quixote* as its paradigm and which accelerates into the modern novel. Although the latter stresses novelty and lets the analytic viewpoint prevail, a longer view would also emphasize the persistence of archetypes, the adaptation of recurrent themes, and the ascendancy of poetry over prose—in short, the continuous unfoldment of the story-telling faculty from primitive myth to *le nouveau roman*.

Thus I am brought to the second of my coordinates: the relation of the past to the present. That literature is the testament of tradition, which orients us to the perspective of time, furnishes us with ever-living patterns of behaviour, and links us directly with our remote progenitors and ultimate progeny—I shall not labour this Arnoldian *topos*, which has served in many an argument on behalf of the humanities. Those who take a strictly formal stance may still resist it, on the grounds that it subordinates pure artistry to the stuff of human experience. Yet even to extract such testimony requires some awareness of the techniques through which it has been transmitted. Conversely, the very closest reading of a text is likely to go astray when it is pursued without reference to the historical context.

Furthermore, I am concerned at this point, not simply with the usefulness of literature as an illustrated supplement to history, but with the convergence of the two, and the constant reshaping of literature by history through the evolution of *genres*. Every *genre* would seem to run its organic cycle. After the long and rich harvest of the novel, latterly we are beginning to ask ourselves whether its season has not been declining. The drama, because of technical requirements, and especially its audiences, has flourished at particular times and places. The remarkable train of circumstance that made it possible for Shakespeare to write his plays is, for me, the central epoch of literary history, and to it I return with perennial enthusiasm in my teaching and in occasional writing.

In the year of Shakespeare's 400th anniversary, I am convinced that he stands nearer to us than he did to his readers and spectators during most of the intervening years. That proximity is partly due to a renewed concentration on him in his natural habitat, the theatre, and partly to the accumulation of studies casting light on his original texts, his rhetorical means, his antiquarian background, and his intellectual climate. Scholars of E. K. Chambers's generation spent industrious and productive careers in gaining public access to the facts, the documents, and the other relevant materials, so that the next generation—

not without gratitude—could undertake to synthesize and interpret with more freedom and more security.

One could set out to be a Renaissance scholar, as I once did,
be deflected by the urgency of more recent manifestations, and
yet not altogether lose touch—I trust—with one's field of pre-
dilection. The gap between scholarship and criticism, which in
the earlier years of our century sometimes took on the aspect of
a quarrel between pedants and dilettantes, has been gradually
closing. The fabric of learning will always need to be filled in
and kept up to date, but today it is relatively well organized.
What with the available editions, works of reference, research
libraries, technological aids, and facilities for travel, the inter-
preter of literature has no excuse for not solidly grounding his
observations or widely testing his speculations. Nor can he
expect to take his bearings, in this increasingly polyglot era,
unless he is at home in more than one language and a venture-
some tourist in several others.

Just as the belatedness of our age has its compensation in
historical consciousness, which can emancipate us from pro-
vinciality in time, so a heightened geographical consciousness
can free us from parochialism in space. My mentor in this
respect was Irving Babbitt, who taught his students to trace
their cultural inheritance back to its Cisatlantic origins. My
third and last coordinate is, therefore, as it must be for any
American who is interested in the arts and in ideas, the span
between the United States and Europe. The tides have ebbed
and flowed appreciably since the days of passionate pilgrims,
innocents abroad, and condescending visitors from England to
America; the approach, from either side, is no longer via dia-
lectic but via dialogue, as the presence of this very deposition
attests.

The immeasurable blessing of having been born into the
English language is perhaps one which a native of another
country may acknowledge without incurring the imputation of
Podsnappery. While remaining aware that his ear may not be
fully attuned to some of the subtle cadences and local associa-

tions of English literature, he would like to think that his visitor's eye could catch a few nuances or discern some analogies which might not have occurred to observers more familiar with the terrain. Again, having had a German-born father, having a Russian-born wife, and having studied and taught on occasion in France, he would almost habitually frame his Anglo-American interests within a broadly European perspective. This orientation has been strengthened by friends and colleagues expatriated westward by the political pressures of our century—I must name, from among them, the late Renato Poggioli.

Looking back, I suppose I should not be surprised at having found a university niche in the hospitably conceived, if awkwardly titled, subject of Comparative Literature; for it is really not so much a subject as an object: an attempt to pool the resources of the variously related literatures, to cross the linguistic barriers that confine them within the framework of national histories, and to provide an area for the consideration of their common features and underlying forces. As attention has tended to shift, in recent years, from reciprocal influences and parallel movements to the permutation of forms and the diffusion of *motifs*, criticism has been accorded more of the scope it needs for rising to a theoretical plane.

Bacon spoke of 'a science pertaining to the imagination', and though no one has developed that conception, it might well emerge from the middle ground between criticism and psychology. Psychoanalysis has thus far been using literature to document its own fascinating inquiries, rather than to illuminate it *per se*. Something more to the purpose might be hoped for from a newer line of investigation which is coming to be known as thematics, whereby the effects of fantasy can be studied through the progressive transformation of images or myths. All this foreshadows a greater emphasis on literature as a process, the component parts of which—even the works of Shakespeare—are subsumed and surpassed by the workings of the whole, as we gradually come to understand it. Needless to say, no one individual or self-limiting group could carry out such a programme; it would demand international co-operation on a high level and in a hopeful future.

However, it does not envisage itself as a school of thought, or urge the adoption of any prescriptive method. Poets, playwrights, and novelists may justifiably venture to found schools, take stands, or issue manifestoes; for they are involved and licensed, committed to experiment or one-sided by design. Critics can scarcely be other than open-minded, unblushingly eclectic rather than doctrinaire, ready to entertain any possibility—to exclude no insight or procedure—that promises to illuminate or enrich the matter at hand. But I am speaking in the optative mood; in practice the exceptions outnumber such rules; and there are too many critics who glory in their one-sidedness. Half-truths are usually more arresting than whole truths, and ignorance can inspire more striking generalizations than a thoughtful canvass of the facts. Since one can never be sure of being absolutely right, why not try to be wrong in an interesting fashion?

Without trading Shakespeare's plays for the laws of thermo-dynamics, criticism would benefit from more rigorous criteria. Possibly the most confusing hazard is the frustrated author who turns critic: either he over-ingeniously rewrites the books he reviews or else, Stanislavsky-like, he identifies himself subjectively with the writers he revaluates. In spite of all the poets who have written effective propaganda for their poetry, there is a good deal to be said for a separation of powers. Wordsworth, after all, was so absorbed in thinking of Burns and Chatterton and himself that he failed to understand the Leech Gatherer's first reply, albeit the second stayed so memorably with him after he departed—leaving the feeble old man to putter on somehow with his humble, old-fashioned, increasingly difficult, thoroughly repellent, and just conceivably therapeutic task.

L. C. KNIGHTS

In Search of Fundamental Values

It is ironic and appropriate that the Editor's request for a statement of critical beliefs and principles should have come at a time when the university year was working towards a climax of activity: ironic, since examiners' meetings, committee meetings, etc., are not conducive to thought about literature; appropriate, since it is only too often in unpropitious circumstances that university teachers, in this country, do what original work they can. What follows is therefore not a formal critical credo; it is simply an attempt to point to those values that shape my own practice as someone who finds it worth while to teach, and sometimes to write about, English literature.

There are many general statements that one could make: for example, literature increases our range of understanding of ourselves, of other people, of our world. But this and similar formulations of the function of literature belong to Coleridge's class of 'truths . . . considered as *so* true, that they lose all the life and efficiency of truth'; they are likely to get no more than a perfunctory nod of recognition. When I cast around for the fundamental value of literature, recognizable in the smallest instance where delight announces its presence and from which all else springs, the point on which the edifice of 'criticism' is raised, I find it in the energy of mind and imagination released by the creative use of words. Wordsworth's 'Sonnet composed upon Westminster Bridge' will serve for an example:

> *Earth has not anything to show more fair;*
> *Dull would he be of soul who could pass by*
> *A sight so touching in its majesty . . .*

The peculiar pleasure of that last line—though the pleasure is independent of conscious recognition of the source—comes from the movement of mind by which we bring together in one apprehension 'touching' and 'majesty': feelings and attitudes springing from our experience of what is young and vulnerable, that we should like to protect, fuse with our sense of things towards which we feel awe, in respect of which it is we who are young, inexperienced or powerless. That is London as Wordsworth saw it on an early autumn morning in 1803 and (to adapt his own words on another occasion) 'planted, for immortality, . . . in the celestial soil of the imagination'. The whole poem grows from a similar fusion of opposites: the buildings momentarily appear as right—as proportioned, inviting and composed—as nature's valleys and hills; the old and shackled city ('Near where the charter'd Thames does flow') is as new as the morning. There is no self-deception: beauty that is 'like a garment' can, we know, be put off; the 'smokeless air' will soon be smoke-filled; and the supreme quiet contains the pulse of life about to resume its course. It is simply that paradox and hyperbole, recognizing themselves for what they are, so activate the mind that, as we read this most beautiful poem, new powers of vision and apprehension come into being.

I am not putting forward the view that paradox is the essential characteristic of poetry: I am simply pointing towards that energizing of the mind that poetry can achieve in an infinity of ways. The exact descriptive word; the surprising figure of speech that levers new recognitions ('Like a green thought . . .'); naked simplicity ('How fast has brother followed brother, From sunshine to the sunless land!'); the alignment of a few objects or events so that the presented experience comes to stand for something as wide as human life itself (Blake's 'Echoing Green' or Frost's 'The Pasture'); slight shifts of tone (as in the last two lines of Frost's 'Come in')—these are only random examples of the ways in which the poet can enlist that active collaboration of the reader through which a specific experience is realized.

I have referred so far to lyric poetry because that is easier to speak of in a short space than prose literature and the longer forms. But whether we read a short lyric, a play, or a novel— supposing each to be good of its kind—the same principles are at work: in varied ways the mind's energies are evoked and directed in a single 'realizing intuition'. In the larger works, of course, the scope is wider and the perceptions are likely to be related in more complex ways. In *King Lear* we not only respond with delight to the ever-changing local realizations— 'Strike flat the thick rotundity of the world' (the reverberations of thunder in a blank verse line); 'women's weapons, water drops' (a range of mistaken assumptions compressed into a phrase)—we bring together the varied and even contradictory meanings of 'need', 'justice', 'folly', and so on, as imagery and action enforce. In this way routine notions and attitudes are broken down, and a new direction of consciousness emerges from the interplay of meanings: not meanings, so to speak, 'out there', as though we were trying to understand a legal document, but meanings in which the reader or spectator is involved as a person, simply because movements of sympathy or antipathy, of assent or dissent—in short, of judgment from a personal centre—are a necessary part of them. A simple example is Lear's assumption that punishment is an essential function of justice:

> *Tremble, thou wretch*
> *That hast within thee undivulged crimes,*
> *Unwhipp'd of justice . . .*

The way we take this is finally determined by our reaction to such things as the picture of the social outcast who is 'whipp'd from tithing to tithing, and stock-punish'd, and imprison'd', and of the 'rascal beadle', society's representative, lashing the whore with her blood on his hands. When the mind really attends to what Shakespeare says or implies about legal justice in *King Lear* it is forced to make strides across the convenient areas of obscurity in which our ignorance and hypocrisy habitually take refuge; it is compelled to make connexions, and its thinking about 'justice', about man's relation to justice, is correspondingly enriched. It is the same with all the other central themes (those who dislike the word are at liberty to use another) of which *King Lear* is composed. Different aspects of experience are held together in what is virtually a single act of attention, and a new direction of thought emerges from the resulting tensions. But because the thinking is in terms of images, not abstract concepts, it is in the fullest possible relation to the intimate personal life of the reader or spectator: the knowledge gained is, as we say, brought home to him—in Keats's phrase, it is 'proved on the pulses'.

The philosopher may raise an eyebrow at the use of 'knowledge' in this context, and indeed there is much defining that even an unphilosophic critic needs to do. I can only say briefly and parenthetically what seem to me the main features of response to literature considered as an activity of knowing. First, what is known is not an object existing independently of the reader: he is himself directly involved in the creative process, and without that involvement there would be no knowledge. In the experience of poetry there is, therefore, a paradoxical union of particularity (we submit to the discipline of what is 'so, and not otherwise') with a spread of meanings that will vary with each individual; for what we have to deal with is not a cut and dried experience, but one that lives and, as it were, reverberates in the receiving mind. That is why literature can so powerfully affect the quality of our relations with the world. Secondly, the knowledge in question can never be completely conceptualized: partly because of the subtle intricacy of the texture of the work (even in a 'classical' work, deliberately avoiding vagueness, there is bound to be a more or less large area of connotation); partly—and more important—because there are, it seems, matters of great concern that can only be known with the co-operation of mental powers below the level of full consciousness. Eliot, like Valéry, has testified that a poem 'may tend to realize itself first as a particular rhythm before it reaches expression in words', and it may be assumed that unless the reader, in turn, is responsive to effects of rhythm that are ultimately unanalysable —as to other non-discursive elements of meaning such as poetic symbols—he will not fully enter into the presented experience. Knowledge of poetry—the knowledge that comes through poetry —demands not only an active but a relaxed and receptive mind.

Attention, collaboration, realization—these are the three basic activities (or, rather, phases or aspects of the same activity) that make up the critical, the fully engaged, response to literature. It is this realizing activity that often makes one want to speak of literature in terms of the depth and presentness of some given object (a person, an action, a landscape), and in a sense one is right to do so: after reading Keats's Ode we do know autumn as never before. But of course there is no object except the poem itself, which, as Susanne Langer insists, offers not ordinary experience but a virtual experience, a symbolic structure of meanings held in the mind. The contradiction, however, is only apparent. When we have undergone the experience of great poetry, of great literature, the world *is* present because the mind, the imagination, is present to the world. It is in this sense that the poet, as Edwin Muir says, releases us from the language—and therefore the world—of the third person and the onlooker, the world of generalities, and continually brings us back to direct confrontation with the particular. The importance of this at a time when, as Muir also points out in his book, *The Estate of Poetry*, so many agencies tempt us to a merely generalized apprehension of life—this needs no stressing. But perhaps it should be added that the sphere of unrealized experience is also the sphere of corrupting fantasy. Literature is a great cleanser, simply because, through language, it energizes the mind. As Coleridge said of Shakespeare's *Venus and Adonis*: 'The reader is forced into too much action to sympathize with the merely passive of our nature.' It was of course also Coleridge who spoke of 'the beneficial after-effects of verbal precision in the preclusion of fanaticism, which masters the feelings more especially by indistinct watch-words'.

It is, then, simply in the growth and strengthening of the imagination that the value of literature resides. Imagination, as I have used the term, is simultaneously the central creative drive of each human being and the organ of all knowledge in which the individual is involved as more than a detached observer. It is an active, relating, realizing power, through which the limited self, with its unlimited desires and its abysmal ignorance of everything that cannot be used or manipulated, grows into a person, freely moving in a world of values and relationships. It is the mediator between the unknown depths within and the so little-known world without. ('Every symbol is two-edged', says Tillich; 'it opens up reality and it opens up the soul.') As a unifying power it simultaneously works towards the integrity and wholeness of the person and the creation of a cosmos from the world of mere experience which, without it, would remain fragmentary and deceptive. The importance of literature is therefore that indicated by Martin Foss when he speaks of 'the work of art . . . giving to everybody and releasing in everybody the power of a creative spiritual life'. But as Foss also reminds us, 'what art brings to the surface is everywhere at work where men think and feel'. Imaginative literature is simply one of the ways through which life comes to consciousness; and the claim that the teacher of literature may justifiably make for his vocation is only possible because what underlies and justifies his activities is what underlies and justifies all the arts and humane studies. To be sure, those who profess other 'subjects' could often, one feels, profit from the insights that a familiarity with literature brings: there is clear profit for the psychologist in Shakespeare and Blake as well as in George Eliot and Henry James; and theologians could perhaps learn something from the symbolic language of great poetry. But then the critic and teacher of literature, in his turn, needs to know something of other ways of eliciting meanings from the world. The study of literature cannot remain self-enclosed. Indeed it is my own conviction—even more now than it was in the days of *Scrutiny*—that there is important work waiting to be done 'on the frontiers', where the study of literature joins hands with the study of history, philosophy, theology, etc. But it will need to be done by those who really know what literature is, not by specialists in other subjects who merely look to literature for documentation.

From what has been said there follow certain practical implications, only one of which can be dealt with here. The job of the teacher of literature calls for a peculiar tact. Just as scholarship, necessary as a tool, can become a barrier between living works and the potentially receptive and responsive mind, so 'practical criticism', an even more urgent necessity in any English course, can inhibit growth from the living centre. Thirty or forty years ago the situation was different; then the need was to free the study of literature from a mere accumulation of dead opinions, fossilized in histories of literature, gilded over with a vague 'appreciation'. The direct confrontation of the pupil with 'the words on the page' was a necessary tactic in a war of liberation. Today one senses danger from the over-anxiety of some teachers to train their pupils in close reading. I hope I shall not be misunderstood on this point: intelligent understanding of literature is what the teacher aims to foster; understanding involves personal judgment; and sensibility can be trained. But intelligence and sensibility may be inhibited by too great a stress on conscious understanding: 'explication' as a formal teaching method can turn the poem into an object almost as effectively as the museum-catalogue techniques of the past. Poetry of any depth may be intuitively apprehended before the experience can be critically defined; wide and voracious reading is as necessary— especially for the young—as the ability to concentrate all one's powers for an hour; and even in the most concentrated act of attention to literature there is a quality of relaxed absorption that makes activity like rest.

GRAHAM HOUGH

The Function of the Imagination

No one has ever put up a statue to a literary critic, as Mr. R. P. Blackmur once ruefully remarked to me; and I do not suppose that anyone has ever set out to become one. Like keeping the streets clean, it is a respectable trade, but one that people drift into rather than choose. Criticism is either the secondary occupation of imaginative writers, or it is the occupation of the middlemen of literature—scholars, teachers and journalists. Literature has need of its middlemen, but they are the diffusers and transmitters of culture, not its creators.

This is the state of the case, now as at all times: but even as I set it down I am conscious of recording a disenchantment—one which I suspect is shared by many people of my age. We who were growing up in the late 1920s into what we hoped would be a literary life were likely to think of criticism as something more than this. We grew up in the next few years into a new literature, and the literature was accompanied by a new criticism. It had to be. The discussions, expositions, expostulations and replies that went on around modern literature in the 1920s and 1930s were necessary means to its absorption.

The new literature was difficult and it seemed at the time to involve some agonizing reappraisals of the old. We needed all the equipment we could get, and we naturally set the importance of this critical activity very high. Most criticism written before 1918 seemed prehistoric, but to the latest kind we gave a very high rank in the intellectual hierarchy. It seemed that a new organon, a whole new range of intellectual apparatus had come into being.

I now believe that this was an illusion. Mr. Eliot's criticism was not a considered re-direction of the literary sensibility; it was a by-product of the development of his own poetry. The science that was to validate I. A. Richards's theory of value never arrived; it was not science; it was not indeed anything. Edmund Wilson's *Axel's Castle* and Leavis's *New Bearings* were valuable pioneer guide-books; but once overtaken by the event their utility quickly evaporated. The peculiar light that seemed to shine from criticism in those days was a borrowed light; its source was not in the critical activity itself but in a stormy sunburst of new creative work. And this is a normal situation.

Criticism serves the creative movement of its time, then for the most part it dies. Since there is always a public to be informed, youth to be educated, new work to be discussed, another criticism will take its place. It will not build on the old, for criticism is not a science; it will simply start again on another tack. The only kind of criticism that constitutes more than a temporary service is that which becomes literature itself, which continues to be read not for its arguments or opinions but as an independent source of literary satisfaction. It is a hard saying for assiduity and learning, but the slightest lyric has a better chance of survival than the most serious critical treatise.

What begins as a commentary on existing literary art may end as a work of art in its own right, and the critic may hope at last to write a handful of essays or a book or two that themselves partake of the nature of literature. But this outcome is hardly under his command; and his only reasonable aim is to serve literature and the understanding of literature in his own time with such honesty and intelligence as he can muster. The classic exposition of this purpose in English is Arnold's essay 'The Function of Criticism at the Present Time'; but classic as it is this piece has always seemed to me to cast its net too wide. Arnold's discussion goes far beyond the limits of criticism; his theme is the whole condition of intellectual health in a society. And this depends on social and historical factors so massive that it cannot properly be handled with the equipment he has at his disposal, still less in literary terms alone. Whoever takes away the sins of the world it is not likely to be a literary critic.

But criticism has its own more limited field of operation. Literature is the memory of a culture, and it is largely by means of criticism, in one form or another, that this memory is kept alive and made generally available. That it should be kept alive is a cultural necessity; but in saying so I do not intend to invoke what is called the inherited wisdom of the past. I would prefer to rest the notion of cultural memory on the grounds finely offered by Sir Herbert Read: 'A mind without memories means a body without sensibility; our memories make our imaginative life.'

This is as true of the body politic as it is of the body natural. It would be particularly inexpedient to draw too heavily on the accumulated wisdom of the past at this moment in history, for we are entered on a phase in which much of it seems no longer to be wisdom, or no longer available to us as such. The prudence of an economics of privation no longer suits an economics of potential plenty; the loyalties of sectarianism and nationalism no longer suit a world that is being painfully forced either into unity or destruction. If we misuse our cultural memory and look to the literature of the past for authority and positive guidance we shall certainly be disappointed. We shall either come back with patterns of life that are no longer successfully lived by any-one, or with something approaching nihilism and despair. The imagination will have to find a new way. But it will only be able to do so if it knows itself, of what it is composed; and it is our cultural memory (largely and most explicitly contained in our literature) that can give us this knowledge.

The one profound truth that we have learnt from modern depth psychology is that nothing is ever lost or superseded in the psychic life. What has long passed from our consciousness as positive belief persists below the surface as image, predisposi-tion and emotional need. It is vital to us to understand these forces. It is vital to know and understand our parents—because they are our parents, not because they were always right. And with the armed forces of change operating at their present strength, this knowledge is in danger of being lost. I believe therefore that the most important business of criticism today is to preserve a continuity, or to re-create one where it has been broken—not for antiquarian reasons, but in order that we may live in the present and meet the future with energies that are properly nourished and firmly based.

Within this general intention there is room for a variety of activities, and a good deal of profitless nagging has come from a failure to admit it. There is room for the scholar-critic who attempts to expound or recall to attention the work of the past, without particular regard to its immediate present interest. There is room for the critic-journalist who is mainly concerned with actualities. Each kind is subject to its own corruptions, and they are often enough exposed, for at present there are signs of a chronic antagonism between them. This is a nuisance, yet it deserves attention; for it has its bearing on the general health of the literary world.

We know that A, getting down to his Monday morning's stint of lectures and tutorials, resents the birdlike freedom of X who seems to fleet away his time in literary cocktail parties and B.B.C. pubs; and that X, aware of his free-lance dependence on capricious literary editors, resents the safe if unmunificent salary enjoyed by A; but leaving the sociology and economics aside we must recognize a genuine difference in their spheres of literary interest. There are two publics for criticism and there are two kinds of criticism in consequence. There is criticism for the general reader—written for a far wider public than ever before, but also for a public that is more hasty, more badgered by immediate current pressures, less inclined to an unhurried contemplation that can take in today and yesterday in the same perspective. With one honourable exception, *The New Yorker*, nothing but a learned journal would now take a literary article as long as one of Sainte-Beuve's *Lundis*. The weeklies are full of stock-market talk and literature is crowded out. Their critical articles are rarely substantial enough to be worth reprinting, and so most of this kind of criticism is condemned to be ephemeral. Yet to the general reader this is what criticism is; for him it is the only means by which literary intelligence is disseminated.

On the other side the scholar-critic is writing for a public increasingly specialized, increasingly professional. There will always be those who are willing to press harder on their literary studies than the intelligent general reader; there will always be those who want to ask more recondite questions, to receive more considered answers and will be willing to digest more learning and more argument in the process. This is a fortunate thing; but what is now a cause for disquiet is that these more exacting readers are increasingly concentrated in the academies, that they form an endless chain of professional literary students and professional literary teachers, consuming each other's products, neither affecting the outer world nor affected by it, and sometimes almost unaware that it exists.

In this state of affairs past literature tends to become the province of the academic, current literature that of the journalist. The split is disastrous, and it should be a serious purpose to reduce its effects. We ought to doubt the authority of a critic who has never shown any concern with the intellectual life of his own day, just as we ought to doubt that of the critic who has confined himself entirely to reviewing current novels. There *is* a criticism that transcends the 'Wain is better than Amis this week' stereotype on the one hand, and 'Thematic Patterns in the Later Eighteenth-Century Sonnet' on the other; but conditions today tend to drive the writer on literary matters to one extreme or the other.

It may be from lack of talent, it may be from lack of opportunity that the difficulty is so rarely overcome; and it is possible that both may be subsumed under lack of determination—the kind of determination that leads the scholar to address not his students alone, but the educated world, and leads the journalist, whatever the limitations of scope and occasion, to utter something beyond the *fadaises* of the moment. Criticism is essentially a co-operative enterprise, as its best practitioners have generally realized: there should be an intellectual community beyond the academic treadmill and the jabber of the coteries. There should be, and at times its outlines can faintly be discerned. To make them more distinct is a far more important object for criticism than any set definition of literary principles.

The critical renaissance of thirty years ago tended to establish certain shibboleths whose value we have since had reason to doubt. I am thinking less of the certifiable utterances of its founding fathers, which were sometimes more cautiously expressed than we recall, than of what succeeded in establishing itself in the general literary mind and in the elaborate process of higher literary education here and in America. One of these was to lay great stress on the impersonal element in literature, on all that could be accounted for by poetical tradition, the state of the language or the availability of a technique. This entailed a corresponding idea of impersonality in literary study. So far as it diverted attention from the love-life of Byron to his actual poetry this was a gain; but there went with it a faith in the virtues of technical analysis that has by now become grotesquely overblown.

'Close reading' and the intent scrutiny of the internal structure of poetry was the great pedagogical weapon of the new criticism; and indeed some of it was wanted. But what began as a remedial measure soon became an end in itself, cut off from history, divorced from all the natural affections and associations of ordinary reading. Thirty years ago it seemed that this mining machinery had brought a new rigour and a new energy to literary study. Now I more than suspect the proliferation of line-by-line analyses of poems, page-by-page examinations of novels by which the academic student of literature is beset. It began with the hope of teaching him to read more effectively; it ends by preventing him from reading anything for himself; criticism is to do it all for him.

So one comes back with relief to a style in criticism that was for a time out of fashion; not indeed to chatter about Harriet Shelley, but to the kind of biographical criticism that can see a work in relation to the whole mental and spiritual life of its author, not to the guide-book facts of literary history, but to criticism that can set a work in its proper ambience or trace an unnoticed pattern of development; to criticism, in short, which is content to put the reader in the way of understanding, to set his imagination on the right track and then leave it to do its own work in its own fashion.

Analogies from machinery, apparatus and technique soon betray us. In reacting against the dominance of personal whim and desultory bookish small-talk we have come near to forgetting that appreciation of the arts is inevitably a personal affair; it depends wholly, in the last resort, on a moment of fusion between the work of art and an individual sensibility that meets it. The quality of our reading can go a little beyond the range of our normal powers. Beyond—or the reading is doing nothing for us; but not far beyond, for no merely literary experience can transform a man, make him into what he is not.

So the quality of criticism is never guaranteed by any efficiency of critical machinery; it depends on the nature of the critic's own mind, and there is much in the structure of our present literary life to prevent us seeing this. In academic criticism technique elaborated beyond any possible use or function; in journalistic criticism a forced brightness that tries to compete with the gossip column or the fashion page; and in both therefore a lack of presence, a lack of authentic human weight, discourse (as Wittgenstein said of high-table conversation) that comes neither from the heart nor from the head. To go beyond this is difficult, and it is not a technical difficulty nor one peculiar to criticism; it is simply the difficulty of all genuine literary utterance. It is often necessary to talk provisionally in terms that express less than our sense of the whole truth; but a critic who persists in a mode of expression that fails to acknowledge the dignity of the poetic imagination is doing violence to his office and his theme. 'This man is hired to depress literature.'

THE FUNCTION OF THE IMAGINATION

The dominant mode of modern literature is what Northrop Frye calls the low mimetic; not low in a social or moral sense, of course, but in the sense that it confines its characters entirely within the limits of actual experience—what we commonly if ineptly call realism. My deepest private allegiance is to a kind of literature, poetry or prose, that assumes a greater degree of imaginative freedom—as most literature did until the rise of the novel. I am inclined to believe that the domination of realism is becoming a weight on our imaginative life. We notoriously lack what other times have found in their poetry—a myth to give coherence and another dimension to daily experience. Yet the reflection of the world as it is can never be enough, and most of us if we are honest must confess that the great myths of the past no longer fit our sense of the world.

There is a kind of criticism abroad today—the kind that makes great work with the concepts of myth, ritual and symbolic tradition—that speaks as though it were the function of imaginative literature to enshrine a body of ancient wisdom by which the initiate is to guide his present course. Some of the writers whom I most admire, Yeats for example, themselves speak in this way, so that it seems ungrateful to assert that they are wrong. I quoted Jung, saying that nothing is ever lost or superseded in the psychic life. But this does not mean, or does not mean to me, that there is a coherent body of occult doctrine lying passively in the past and waiting to be discovered. Here we could quote Yeats against himself:

> *I mock Plotinus' thought*
> *And cry in Plato's teeth,*
> *Death and life were not*
> *Till man made up the whole,*
> *Made lock, stock and barrel*
> *Out of his bitter soul.*

If the highest purpose of literature is to create an acceptable and livable myth, this must be a continuing purpose. It cannot be fulfilled by destroying the myths of the past and erecting some gimcrack skyscraper on the shifting rubble. Nor can it be fulfilled by reverent or superstitious restoration. The historic work of the literary imagination can only be continued by understanding and accepting the myths of the past, because they are part of our being; and by making, out of that knowledge yet extending beyond it, a new myth which is as yet only a part of our being because we can catch dim and intermittent glimpses of it.

This may seem a grandiose note to end on; but I do not believe that our literature or our criticism can amount to much unless some such idea can be felt to preside distantly over our imaginative activities, however scattered, fragmentary or individually unimportant they may appear.

F. R. LEAVIS

Research in English

━━━━━━━━━━━━━ ◆⋙∘⋘◆ ━━━━━━━━━━━━━

I read in *The Times Literary Supplement* for 28 June the leading article entitled 'Tangible Results' and felt a strong
impulse to write and express my gratitude. When I started
to act on the impulse I soon found myself in difficulties. Correspondence printed in the succeeding issue confirmed both my
sense that the opportunity I had seen the article as presenting
ought to be taken and my realization that the taking would not
be such a simple matter of direct comment as would lend itself to
the necessary brevity of a letter.

'Perhaps the time is ripe for some research into the nature of
literary research': when I read this closing suggestion of the
letter printed from Mr. Philip Hobsbaum I was moved to something that might be called assent. But I saw that he didn't really
share the conviction that had been troubling me, a strong sense
of the grounds for which (and of the urgent need to get recognition for them) being my own response to the article in *The
Times Literary Supplement*: the conviction that it is high time for
some thinking about the nature of 'research' as it should be
understood in university English Schools. I intimate in this last
clause my view that the right answers to the questions that need
to be asked will hardly be arrived at unless the inquiry into the
nature of 'literary research' subserves—and is thought of as
subserving—a concern for an adequate conception of liberal
education and the university.

What made it clear to me that Mr. Hobsbaum didn't share at
any rate the intensity of my conviction was his general optim-

ism. The review accompanying the leading article and providing its occasion had dealt with some depressingly futile products of the American academic industry. Referring to it, Mr. Hobsbaum remarked that the 'reviewer . . . was probably attacking something already dead'. 'That is too easily said' gives my reaction to that comment. I mean, there *is* a menacing academicism against which we have to be militantly upon our guard—a form of academicism institutionally established and invincible in America, and one the tendency towards which in this country— the developments of civilization favouring it—is much strengthened by American influence (so many of our politically dominant academics and our 'coming' younger ones have spent some time at American universities). The apprehension I express—and I know I am not alone in feeling it—is not to be dismissed by the reminder that there have been good books written as theses for the Cambridge Ph.D., or the assurance that we are unlikely to have a proliferation of the blankly or brutally crass kinds of doctoral manufacture here.

Whatever there may be to be said about the reminder or the assurance, I myself have, for the past dozen years or so, watched a pertinacious drive to establish in Cambridge 'English' what I may properly call the American idea of research and its place in university education. Such a drive—a drive (one to be feared and fought) for such an end—could hardly in those early days of the Ph.D., forty-odd years ago, when the English Tripos was finding and asserting its distinctive character, have been thought of as possible. No one supposed that research in relation to the English School could be anything analogous in status and essential importance to what it was in relation to the scientific departments.

The Ph.D., we gathered, had been instituted with an eye to the expectations of young American graduates who might be expected in the future to contemplate coming to England instead of going to Germany. By a kind of accident (it seemed—for Balfour, or whoever had promoted the idea, would hardly have thought of the critical study of English literature, to which we were committed, as a relevant academic field), we too, we of the English Tripos, had the benefit of this new institution, Ph.D. research. And we quickly established an implicit understanding of the way in which it could be made truly a benefit; in ten or a dozen years we had established the appropriate tradition. (I say 'we', a suitably indeterminate word, suggesting as it does the unofficial, informal and non-authoritative: the thing was not done by way of committees, reports, boards or re-formulated regulations.) 'Research' in English was seen as providing opportunities for men and women who had distinguished themselves in the English Tripos to go on with their education and the discovery of their interests and powers, learn how to carry through a sustained piece of constructive thinking in the exploration of some congenial theme or field, and, in short, to improve their qualifications for discussing literature with intelligent undergraduates—helping them to conduct their studies profitably and to make the most of their opportunities.

This was the simple direct account to be given, we thought, of 'research' in English—the short answer to the question, how was its place in the scheme of things to be thought of. But of course a comprehensive account would have entailed a good deal more, and raised a certain complexity of considerations. When, by way of intimating what these were, I invoke *Scrutiny*, I bring out the force of my 'we'. There are two statements to be made with immediate point: (i) *Fiction and the Reading Public*, which was written as a doctoral thesis in the English School, was a major relevant fact behind the founding of *Scrutiny*; (ii) *Scrutiny* emerged out of the informal gatherings ('social'—in the pursuit of their intellectual interests) of a number of research students round a friendly hearth.

If there had not been the English Tripos, with the consequent notion of 'research' that represents its ethos at the level of post-graduate studies, there would have been no *Scrutiny*. The *Scrutiny* group, in fact, in the days when the new enterprise was being engendered and founded, had much to do with the establishing of the distinctive Cambridge tradition of 'research' in

English—as even a relaxed turning-over of the volumes will make pretty clear. A number of those who frequented the milieu had subjects that may fairly be said to have been inspired by *Fiction and the Reading Public*. In fact, had not authority at the centre of power in the English School detected an illicit influence and, resolving that this kind of thing must not be allowed to go on, made its will to be discouraging very plain, Cambridge would before the war have unmistakably had a 'school', if an unofficial one, of what is nowadays conveniently referred to as 'literary sociology'.

I am not meaning to suggest that we thought of all 'research' as being of that kind; very much the contrary. The stress fell on 'literature' and 'criticism': our concern was for kinds of study in which, though they might not perhaps be classifiable under literary criticism, the part of the literary-critical intelligence should be essential and fundamental. And such study, much stimulated and nourished by *Scrutiny* (for all the official non-existence of that offending insistence of life) went on at Cambridge. Its product, direct and indirect, is to be seen on a large scale in the volumes of *Scrutiny*.

I refer to *Scrutiny* in this way because to do so is essential to the key point I have to make. It is agreed, I hope, that, as Mr. Hobsbaum suggested, there has been a need for some thinking about the nature of 'research' in English. It is plain, for instance, that, for our purposes, the phrase 'a genuine contribution to knowledge' has a marked infelicity, and that research in relation to an English School can have no close analogy with research in the sciences. On the other hand, 'research' properly conceived (there is a convenience in retaining the term) has nevertheless an essential part to play if the English School is to be that which it should be: that which, generating in the university a 'centre of human consciousness—perception, knowledge, judgment and responsibility', should make it really a university; that is, more than a collocation of specialist departments. 'It is assumed', I said in my Richmond lecture, *Two Cultures?* (for the sake of economy I will permit myself a further brief quotation—the context can be examined by anyone interested enough),

'that work in the scientific departments must be in close touch with the experimental-creative front. In the same way, for the university English School there is a creative front with which, in its function and nature, the School must be in the closest relation. I am not thinking of the fashionable idea that the right qualification for a teaching post is to be a poet—or a commercially successful novelist. I am thinking of what *Scrutiny* stood —and stands for: of the creative work it did on the contemporary intellectual-cultural frontier in maintaining the critical function.'

The point that I am insisting on is that the governing conception of 'research' we need in English will not be arrived at by trying to find some suitable formula that will serve better than 'genuine contribution to knowledge' to describe the good thesis. There are clearly a number of acceptable kinds. Research has to be thought of in relation to the whole 'idea' of the university English School. The representative research student (there is a good deal of point in thinking in terms of *him*—or *her*) should be a person of some distinction of mind and exceptional enterprise and self-reliance, capable of proposing for himself a sustained piece of work worth doing and of carrying it through, whose presence in the community clearly tends to strengthen it as the milieu of creative intercourse it ought to be.

For it is only in terms of maintaining and strengthening the life of such a community that the educational problem itself—the university's problem of humane education—can be seriously thought about without something like despair. Of course, to have an intelligently conceived syllabus or field of study, free from wasteful or frustrating requirements, for the student—that matters to him directly in the most obvious way. It matters to him also, and not less, by way of its mattering so much to his teachers and guides, and it matters to them in making it possible for mature minds capable of first-hand judgment and creative thought to pursue the development of their interests on the frontiers while at the same time (the better teachers for it) drawing stimulus from their 'teaching' and from their contacts in general with undergraduates—representatives of lively, expectant and disinterested intelligence.

It is partly the role of research students to be among those senior members of the community, and, in close touch as they are with the younger world, they have an essential liaison function. It matters to them, too, and in the same way (with advantage again at the undergraduate level) that there should be intelligent teaching for them to do. They are, in fact, a necessary element in the total community that 'English' in a university ought to be—must be, if 'English' is to perform its function as central humanity, and count at all significantly in relation to the sciences: the community that makes it possible for the undergraduate member to get the higher education that cannot, when we inquire into its nature and possibilities, be adequately suggested in terms merely of syllabus and kinds of instruction. My stress falls generally on the collaborative total interplay that constitutes the 'community' and particularly on the necessary part in it of the research student (the right kind of research student), if work in the English School is to answer seriously to an account of it as 'in touch with the creative front'.

There is a battle to be fought everywhere, and, as I have said, in this matter of research it clearly has to be fought at Cambridge. The living actual tradition of research from which Cambridge 'English' benefited so much was tacit and informal. The drive I refer to is calculated, concerted and pertinacious and aims at new official and institutional provision—amounting, in fact, to the establishing of something in the nature of the American Graduate School. Its promoters have a habit (and one's pointing out that there is no valid comparison does not seem to trouble them) of producing statistics to show how much greater is the percentage of research students at American universities than at Cambridge. But the argument starts on a humane note —a note of compassionate concern for the hordes of depressed research students who have been admitted to research in English, but just cannot get on, and need *much* more help. I have found that all the intelligent research students I meet recoil from the idea of having to have such help and evade the campaigning and self-proffering helpers as much as they dare.

The scale on which research students are to be assumed in future to need help is intimated in the proposal that a University Lecturer who carries the burden of 'looking after' half a dozen research students should be let off one of the courses of lectures for which he is salaried. One's comment is that a graduate who needs that amount of help should never have been admitted as a research student. Positively, one invokes the hitherto unquestioned criterion: the type research student should be the First Class Tripos man, judged to be capable of sustained independence and self-direction, and needing in the matter of help only a standing relation with a congenial senior to whom he can go now and then for criticism and advice. The reply one gets is a polite bow to the superannuated ideal, and a recall to realism. The university has a new duty, we are told: there is a besieging host, ever-increasing, of Indians, Africans, Commonwealth people in general, Levantines, who aspire to become university teachers of English literature, and must therefore have a Ph.D. —preferably a Cambridge one (though it is admitted that a large proportion of them couldn't hope to take the English Tripos with much credit—even if they could pass).

In this reply the significance of the drive is plainly avowed. And the rejoinder is clear and unanswerable: no alleged new duty can abrogate the duty of Cambridge to maintain the standard. No one questions that in respect of the sciences, and it holds no less of 'English'. Of course, in 'English' the problems of defining the nature of standards, getting recognition for them, and ensuring enforcement are harder. And that makes the burden of responsibility resting on Cambridge the heavier—for reasons of history, which have given Cambridge some advantages, so that it is reasonable to fear that if the standard is not maintained there it won't be anywhere. I am thinking of the inimical pressures which are everywhere insistent and insidious.

G   97

To debase 'research' in the way proposed is not merely to deprive the 'community' of which I have spoken of an essential element of life. Those concerned for the English School at any university should recognize clearly that if they permit anything of the kind there will be general disastrous concomitants, and that the corruption entailed in conniving (and more than conniving) at the sending out as highly qualified university teachers people who are very far from being that, and often grossly unfit —sending them out with a hallmark to which they have no right —will have a general corrupting influence. They should stand firm on the principle that a research student should be a distinguished mind, with exceptional enterprise and self-reliance, and that the mark of the genuine research student is that he has something he wants to do. But the specialized director of research, with his card-index from which he is ready to hand out subjects—*he* will certainly come with the kind of regime proposed, and he will be a centre of blight. For he will remain in the English School, he will be felt in the prevailing ethos, he will still be a university teacher, and he will examine as well as instruct undergraduates.

Whatever is to be done for the sub-standard would-be researcher, towards whom it is felt we have a duty, there must be a resolute and uncompromising concern to ensure that standards are in no way prejudiced and the rights of the genuine research student are not touched. That will be difficult, but it is surely plain that any solution by compromise will be stultifying.

The desperate need today is that 'English' should justify the claim it is committed to making: that it provides something real and irreplaceable, a discipline unequivocally genuine and deserving the respect of scientists.

Part II

RAYMOND PICARD

Critical Trends in France

————————◇➣◦➢◇————————

M odern English and American criticism, let us admit it, is very little known in France, where its influence can be regarded as practically nil. Modern French criticism for that matter is hardly more known in England or America. Thus in so important an American work on the New Criticism as Wellek and Warren's *Theory of Literature* (second edition, 1955), the bibliography of over 700 titles includes neither Jean Paulhan's *Fleurs de Tarbes* nor Claude-Edmonde Magny's *Sandales d'Empédocle*, though these undoubtedly rank amongst the most remarkable critical works published in France during the last twenty-five years. Leaving that aside, however, French ignorance of modern English and American critical attitudes is on the face of it surprising when we consider the enormous public which exists on all levels for Anglo-American literature. D. H. Lawrence and Faulkner are part of the heritage of the average French reader: why then should he be unaware of the critics who were their contemporaries? It took Shakespeare 150 years to cross the Channel (and in what a state he arrived!). Nowadays, when it takes Albee only 150 days to cross the Atlantic, why don't the modern critics come with him?

The first point is that far fewer people are interested in criticism. The reader who is really concerned about the standards he uses in choosing and judging books is a reader apart. Whereas a novel may appeal to an immense public, a critical study is only intended for that limited number who really wish to think about and plan their reading, in other words for those engaged in teaching literature, for intellectuals and literary critics. That being the case, and publishers not being heroes, it is only natural that works of this kind will rarely justify the expense of translation. They are available in English of course, but the French public capable of reading them is even smaller than the English and American public that can perform the reciprocal feat. Moreover the examples considered in such works will be taken almost entirely from the field of English literature —in the work mentioned above, for example, there are two references to Boileau as against twenty-three to Pope—and English literature is often little known to French readers. Lastly there is a widespread belief that a school of criticism is more or less bound up with the literature that provides its problems: that the critical methods appropriate to Shakespeare, Coleridge or Meredith, for instance, will not be valid for Racine, Lamartine, or Huysmans. Rightly or wrongly it is believed that for the literature of any nation there are corresponding national methods of criticism. This is particularly the case in France, which has an old and robust (even if sometimes inadequate) tradition of criticism, a body of work in which remarkably few ideas have ever been borrowed from any criticism abroad and applied to French literature. The old-established superiority complex of the French in the field of ideology and philosophy seems to forbid their importing critical concepts for the better understanding of their own literature.

They would do well, however, to ponder the Anglo-American example, which would make them more conscious of the problems inherent in their criticism and show them that some of their aims and reactions are not without analogies elsewhere. French criticism is in the throes of a grave crisis, all the more grave for lying beneath the surface and for manifesting itself in facts rather than in people's minds. Should criticism exist? What should be its object? What should be its methods? The situation is so confused, the blind clinging to tradition so overpowering, and the indifference of a large section of the public so complete, that no one thinks of asking, no one dares to ask, such questions.

The daily output of books nowadays is so enormous that the literary critics of our newspapers have the choice of being ascetics or charlatans, though in fact they are for the most part somewhere between the two. Often lacking any real scholarship, they have the same tendency as I have observed in America too to confine their interests to modern literature. For them, French literature begins with Rimbaud: in fact one of them a few years ago asked me quite seriously: 'Is *La Princesse de Clèves* worth reading?' Those who teach literature have read the classics, but they are no longer certain what they ought to teach. Should it be the lives of writers, the literary history of the age in question (in the same way as economic history is taught), the history of ideas, the philosophy of the art of writing, the psychology of authors or their characters, the birth of literary creation, the philology of poetic diction, or what? Critical studies do in fact tackle all these subjects and many others as well.

A movement has started, however, a somewhat negative but by no means insignificant one, against the exaggerated practice of biographical criticism so firmly entrenched in France, and in favour of a return to the work itself, as is the tendency in present-day Anglo-Saxon criticism. It has at last been grasped that the life of a writer does little to explain his work, and that circumstantial anecdotes about creation shed little light upon the act of creation itself, still less upon the resulting work. The old object lesson of the apple tree producing apples, which the nineteenth-century critical school saw as the perfect explanation, only makes the darkness deeper, for the mystery of creation and the significance of the apple remain totally unexplained, and there is, if one reflects a moment, nothing that could be called a *reason* why an apple tree should not produce pears or apricots. Sainte-Beuve was more responsible than anyone for this confusion of the life and work of an author, yet the odd thing is his prestige is still intact; the epicene Sainte-Beuve, toying with literature, who in his time accomplished the feat of totally misjudging Balzac, Hugo, Stendhal, Tocqueville, and Baudelaire, is still the patron saint of most French critics. In fact this radical separation of a writer's work from the writer himself, which personally I think to be desirable in a great many cases, and which accident has enforced in the case of Homer, Lucretius, and Shakespeare, is still far from being generally accepted in France.

There are several reasons for this. First of all, people adore biographies, which they generally find much more intriguing than the works of the man they are reading about; moreover they are simple enough to believe that an author has put into his work those homely adventures which his biographer has imagined or discovered in his life. The taste for historical gossip, for curious and preferably scandalous details, is so avid that it needs nothing short of heroism on the part of the critic if he is to brush them aside altogether. All the more so because Proust, for instance, although decrying Sainte-Beuve, pointed out the deep human significance of the slightest anecdote, the most trifling *concierge* gossip. Thus consideration of the author himself remains important, though for motives that are nowadays called psychological. The psycho-analytical critic will probe the behaviour and attitude of an author for signs of this complex or that. With the complexes paraded, the work can easily be shown to be the expression, more or less obsessional, of the author's psychology. One of the more disastrous examples of this diagnostic approach is provided by Jean-Paul Sartre's study of Baudelaire, which admirably reconstructs the poet's psychology but does nothing to explain how or why he did in fact come to write precisely *Les Fleurs du Mal*, nor what *Les Fleurs du Mal* are. It is not difficult to see what hopelessly arbitrary and unreal fantasies such criticism can lead to when writers who have been dead for centuries, and the circumstances of whose lives are little known, are laid on the psycho-analyst's couch, the more so as very few of the critics will have Sartre's talents as a psychologist.

Turning from those who wallow in anecdotes or abandon themselves to the giddy flights of psycho-analysis, we find amongst French critics more subtle ways of pursuing biographical criticism, even though it may be ostensibly repudiated.

The admittedly interesting business of studying a writer's basic intuitions, the structure of his thought and the quality of his sensibility, often leads critics to place on the same level and even to fuse into a vague general concept, elements discerned in the historical personality of the writer, on the one hand, and those revealed in his literary production on the other; so that once again we have a confusion of the man and his work. What has come to be called *intentionnalité* (roughly the question of a man's general outlook), seems to me an ambiguous and even dangerous notion, and unconscious *intentionnalité* still more so. It is valid to the extent to which it enables us to define the spirit of a work in terms of an aim which that same work fulfils, transcends and betrays, all in one; it is dangerous when it draws its premises and its pseudo-justifications in a more or less arbitary psychology of the author, thought up by the critic.

For my part I remain resolutely hostile to biographical criticism, except perhaps when it reveals the author's attitude to social problems and thus contributes to the sociological study of literature. What shocks me most in recent contributions to the subject—particularly the most seductive ones—is that the literary work itself is reduced to a mere pretext for a psychological or philosophical essay which in effect passes beyond it. The aim here is to comment on the human condition, to disclose a particular metaphysical or psychological perspective (the critic's own), to study the phenomenon of literary creation in general, but not to explain the work. The critics claim to be going back to the text, but they are treating it as a reservoir of documents, symptoms and signs of all sorts; they see in the text only what is beyond or further, the *project*; in other words they treat it all as a more or less necessary step to something else. Such criticism as this does not seem to me to deserve the name *literary*. It takes its illustrations and its jumping-off point from literature, that is all, and had much better be called psychology, anthropology, phenomenology, or whatever it really is. It betrays its lack of real interest in literature by putting all written matter on the same level, so that a private note scribbled in haste ranks with a published text which is part of a carefully organized body of work. Since it is their testimony, psychological or otherwise, that matters, their literary merits hardly count. No attention is given to a work's composition or to its architecture; everything that comes from the author is ground down to a rubble of signs, undifferentiated by any literary judgment. If some of the champions of this kind of criticism claim to be interested in 'structure', their structure is certainly not a literary one.

One of the most dangerous tendencies to which contemporary criticism is subject is thus to deviate from literature. Against that I have myself always considered that the first duty of the literary critic is to focus all his attention on the literary work, which I regard as an end in itself, complete and absolute. Like many Anglo-Saxons, I believe in studying literature from the inside, concentrating on its intrinsic qualities. Naturally it would be a mistake to neglect the environment or the social conditions: the historical meaning should not be ignored, not that it need necessarily be agreed with. But the critic must always return to the work itself and to the literary universe to which it belongs while still constituting an autonomous and self-justifying unit. For a work, be it poem or novel, is sufficient unto itself, endowed with its own power and containing its own clues. These are to be found simply by examining the text: criticism begins and ends above all as textual elucidation, as *explication de texte.*

What is there to elucidate? It is the peculiar property of literature to be able at the same time to excite an aesthetic pleasure and to communicate an intellectual message. Of all the arts it is the most intellectual in its expression, and of all intellectual activities it is the most artistic. The mystery of poetry lies precisely in its ability to bring together sound and sense, philosophy and music; and all literature is to some extent poetry. Thus the critic is beset with danger on either hand. The aesthete will be satisfied with a formalist criticism which brings out beauties of rhythm and language, regardless of meaning. The philosopher will search only for the meaning, and beauty itself will only provide him with elements for some kind of diagnosis.

If philosophy tends nowadays to become confused with literature, that is no reason why literature should allow itself to
become confused with philosophy, nor literary criticism with
philosophic criticism. If criticism is to be worth anything it must
be complete, and accordingly we have to establish the idea of
literary meaning. In studying the inherent structure of the work,
the interweaving of themes, and the economy of development,
the critic must reveal, in the poise and tension of the edifice, an
architecture that is both graceful and demonstrative. This concrete rhetoric is best understood in relation to certain literary
archetypes which it has helped to shape: we need to reintroduce
the *critique des genres* (what Wellek calls 'literary *kind*'). Moreover, and this is the second point, the technical study of the work
should be accompanied by a psychology—which such study both
explains and vindicates—dealing with the work's effects upon
the reader. The work only acquires reality in the mind which
lives it, in which it becomes an irreplaceable experience. The
object of criticism is to enrich this experience by giving it an
objective basis; an intelligible relation must be established between the work, in its inward coherence, and the effects it has on
the psychology of the reader for whom it is intended.

So the critic has no reason to retreat into an unhealthy
humility. Of course he must respect the integrity and the specific
value of the work he is studying, and not consider it as material
for his own expatiations. But neither must he underestimate his
task or withdraw into his usual inferiority complex in face of the
creative mind. After all, if his role, is as we have seen, to be a
'good reader', it is for him that books are written. The writer
needs a public to fulfil himself, or at least to justify himself;
there is a problem of production in literature, and it is far from
being merely an economic one. The critic represents the con-
sumers. It is he who is nourished by books, who savours them
and appreciates them. But it is a difficult business to enjoy and
to be the judge of your enjoyment, to be a taster of literature
without ceasing to love it too.

HANS MAYER

Critics and the Separation of Powers

'In spite of all the poets who have written effective propaganda for their poetry, there is a good deal to be said for a separation of powers.' HARRY LEVIN

Of course Dr. Levin is right. The failed or disgruntled writer, who turns critic in order either to give his own version of his confrères' work or else to condemn it because it isn't written as he himself would have written it, is not unknown in German literary history either. One can think of some well-known names. Christian Dietrich Grabbe, for instance wrote an absurdly silly essay in 1827 called 'The Craze for Shakespeare', in which he set out to persuade his German readers that Shakespeare was a very feeble playwright who took much less trouble about his writing than a man like Schiller. Luckily Grabbe had more sense than to obey his own critical principles, and his own plays are inevitably influenced less by Schiller than by Shakespeare. Just the opposite line was taken some twenty years later by Otto Ludwig, who sacrificed Schiller to the Shakespeare cult and turned out endless Shakespeare imitations, most of them sterile enough, where he tried to find the formula for plays like *Macbeth* by identifying himself as closely as possible with their author. The only result was that no German theatre today will perform his works.

Those are two horrid examples of the kind of muddle that occurs when real writers try to act as critics in the same way as reviewers who never want to be anything else. Nor is it only literature where this applies. In music, for instance, one has the really laughable rubbish which a great man like Hugo Wolf could write in an effort to demolish the new symphonies of Brahms.

Are we therefore, as Dr. Levin suggests, to adopt the principle of the separation of the powers as a basic condition of good criticism? That is the real problem. Moreover, which part is the critic to play within that separation? Is his power to be legislative, executive or judicial? Confining ourselves to German literary history alone (though so far as I can see there have been similar instances in most European literatures), we can find examples of all three. Each had its moment of glory. That moment is everywhere past. Thus from the Renaissance up to the Enlightenment it was generally agreed that the critic must act as a judge. It was his job to try new works and see if they fulfilled the rules of aesthetics and poetics as they had supposedly been handed down from former ages. As late as Lessing's day this was the principle; Aristotle was his touchstone for the testing of all new dramatic works. Not that Lessing was fussy about details; he got over his particular fondness for Shakespeare by blandly proclaiming him a perfect example of the Aristotelian school. But by about 1770 this critical standpoint had become untenable; and in our own time we have seen Bertolt Brecht applying all his genius as a playwright and all his sharpness as a thinker to establishing the need for a 'non-Aristotelian dramaturgy and drama'. Once the laws of aesthetics were overthrown the critic's judicial power was finished.

German classicism as embodied in Goethe and Schiller then turned the critic into a legislator. These two writers were exceptional in that they were critics of real importance; Benedetto Croce even said jokingly that he was prepared to acknowledge Schiller's criticism while banishing the poet to the limbo of 'unpoetry'. Yet it cannot seriously be maintained that the aesthetic principles of German classicism have any legislative force left in them now. Only in the socialist countries are there still those who insist that the socialist literature of the future must develop

on the basis of classical standards, on the grounds that classicism, especially that of Goethe, represents the culminating point
of the bourgeoisie's aesthetic awareness at a time when it was
still a rising class. This has always been Georg Lukács's view,
though it cannot exactly be said that its literary results prove the
vitality of those aesthetic rules which were worked out in
Weimar between 1795 and 1805. Nor can it be maintained that
Lukács's critical application of those rules has been entirely
happy. It led to an intellectually impossible antithesis: Thomas
Mann or Franz Kafka; opening the door to the author of *Dr.
Faustus* while the writer from Prague was thrown out as decadent. All this in the name of a criticism based on classical
standards.

It was a sad day for German literature when Romantics like
Friedrich Schlegel and Novalis revolted against Weimar classicism and declared that the critic must assume executive power;
in future he would have to write all the *belles-lettres* himself. This
was the start of that terrible theory by which criticism itself has
to become a work of art: poetry engendered by the contemplation of poetry. The effect on ordinary newspaper criticism was a
dreadful, sticky, sentimental, critical gush; works were not so
much reviewed as serenaded. This abuse was elevated to a
political virtue under Dr. Goebbels and the Third Reich.
Hitler's Minister of Propaganda was so incensed by the sur-
viving remnants of art and literary criticism that he banned them
out of hand and only permitted so-called *Kunstbetrachtung*, liter-
ally the observation of art. Criticism gave way to pure serenade.
Yet even a gifted writer like Alfred Kerr, a self-proclaimed
follower of the German Romantics, clung to this aesthetic superstition which insists that the critic is himself an original writer.
Kerr would repeatedly and aggressively maintain that the subject of his critiques was quite unimportant; all that mattered was
the fact that he, Alfred Kerr, had come on some new book or
play which gave him a pretext for a piece of critical fine writing.
This is where opposites meet. Alfred Kerr in Berlin and Karl
Kraus the Viennese critic were bitter enemies. Kraus too how-

ever saw himself as a critical belle-lettrist or a belle-lettristical critic.

We are back where we started. The critic has operated as judge, legislator, prime minister, and here we are again with the sterile hybrid of critic and original writer. So can one really say that the separation of the powers has been worth it? Only perhaps in the negative sense that we have come to see that any attempt to give the critic a definite function in the literary field comes up against practical difficulties. We have got out of the way of looking respectfully up to Aristotle. We are men of the twentieth century trying, in our capacity as critics and as human beings who have been through one or in many cases two world wars, to cut a road through to Goethe's writing without paying too much attention to his aesthetics. Nothing makes us more suspicious than when critics indulge in that spurious poetry which is achieved at the expense of clarity and often enough of honesty too.

So what critical principles ought to guide us? I read Dr. Steiner's essay on 'Humane Literacy' with great interest and much inward agreement, but I wonder if he is right in thinking it possible to draw a clear distinction between the literary historian's and the literary critic's methods of working. It is not enough to refer to the care with which the historian or philologist interprets a text, for any criticism of literature that cannot place a text historically and interpret it structurally is quite simply bad criticism. Conversely I would say, after a fair amount of experience professing literary history at a university, that research in my subject is bound to be futile unless it is concerned to help the young to gain access to the works of the past from experience of our own time. At the 1947 Zurich P.E.N. Congress Thomas Mann lectured on 'Nietzsche's Philosophy in the Light of our Experience'. I don't think either the literary historian or the literary critic nowadays can interpret works, whether of contemporary literature or of the past, without making an effort to set them in this 'light of our experience'. 'We cannot pretend that Belsen is irrelevant to the responsible life of the imagination', says Dr. Steiner. He is absolutely right, and what he says applies to the literary historian quite as much as to the critic. Here in Germany neither the member of an English seminar nor the theatre critic can in future treat *The Merchant of Venice* naively as pure literary material. Nor can one act as if Richard Wagner's antisemitic writings and Rilke's letters in praise of Mussolini had never been written.

What is the right attitude for the critic today? The Editor of *The Times Literary Supplement* has kindly asked me to review my methods of work as a critic and literary historian, and to start by deciding whether or not modern English and American literature has had any influence on them. This invitation comes at a very suitable moment, for I had already felt like replying some weeks ago on quite a different occasion. My American colleague Dr. Demetz had reviewed a work on the New Criticism by an East Berlin Marxist scholar in a Hamburg paper, approving his choice of theme on the slightly ironical grounds that critics such as Georg Lukács and Hans Mayer had hitherto recognized virtually nothing outside German literature apart from the French literary tradition and the classical heritage. This is largely so, but he was not entirely right where I am concerned. There is no room here to discuss how far I have been affected by English and American literature; I can but refer readers to my own works, with the reminder perhaps that it can hardly have been pure accident that made me write successive studies of Fielding, Smollett and Sterne some ten years ago. But what about Anglo-Saxon criticism?

I must confess that its influence has in the main been negative. My way of judging literary works was sharply opposed from the first to the principles of T. S. Eliot, and if I were to say today which method struck me as most remote from my own way of working I would say the New Criticism. Right from the start I found my relationship with works of literature conflicting with such sayings of Eliot's as that 'A literary critic should have no emotions except those immediately provoked by a work of art', or 'Honest criticism and sensitive appreciation are directed not upon the poet but upon the poetry'. This always struck me as a method which broke its own rules, for Eliot and his successors are quite aware of all the historical facts relating to the composition of the work in question, to the writer's life and to the historical background. Officially such awareness is banished as being impure, but as soon as the New Criticism gets down to work the back door swings open and it is readmitted none the less.

Against that, I was greatly interested by the critical writings of Edmund Wilson and Richard Hoggart. Am I then to admit that the Anglo-Saxon outlook on literature has contributed something to my own methods of work? Less in the treatment of contemporary works perhaps than where literary-historical research is concerned. At a time when a number of literary scholars in Germany and Switzerland stand for a kind of New Criticism called *Dichtungswissenschaft*, or Science of Literature, which is to take the place of old-style history of literature, I have again and again been glad to see my colleagues in the German departments of British and American universities laying stress on the study of an author's life and times and hesitating to embark on any interpretation not grounded on thorough historical knowledge.

There is, however, the question of how such historical relationships are to be interpreted. This is where I differ from many of my Anglo-Saxon colleagues (though not from all), in that I have learnt a great deal from Georg Lukács. I am not content to study historical facts without trying to interpret them as relationships; nor do I think that the history of European literature over the past 200 years can be understood unless one looks for the various phases in the evolution of bourgeois society that underlie it. In most cases, admittedly, Lukács found it enough to spot the symptoms of social progress or 'ideological decline' (*ideologischer Verfall*) in specific works of Goethe or Thomas Mann, Balzac or Flaubert. But as the Editor has asked me if my own critical principles have developed at all in the course of my work I am bound to say that my methods have tended to become

increasingly independent of Lukács's. I cannot accept any longer
his way of explaining a work of art's relationship to its historical
background without taking into account any of those details that
make it a work of art. To some extent the same historical experiences underlie any of Goethe's novels; but I can't help inter-
preting *Werther* differently from *Elective Affinities*.

It must be admitted that a lot of aesthetic principles which are
obviously still valid for Lukács have, in my own experience,
come to seem unrewarding. I cannot see that making a distinction between socialist and critical realism has led to the erection
of any truly reputable standards by which to view European
literary history. Like Brecht, who also disagreed with Lukács on
this point, I furthermore feel that the concepts of realism and
popularity (*Volkstümlichkeit*) have proved unhelpful to scholars.
Not to mention such dubious notions as *Parteilichkeit*, or party
point of view, which in practice results in theology rather than
criticism. It would be fair to say that in my efforts to understand
works of literature and explain them I was at first influenced
mainly by Thomas Mann and Georg Lukács. This was then use-
fully offset by my acquaintanceship with Brecht. But perhaps we
may now have reached a point where it is permissible to wonder
whether Brecht in his literary criticism achieved anything more
than propaganda for his own writings, even though he himself
honestly believed he had established critical principles for the
whole of future literature.

There are, however, one or two things which I think my work
as a critic has taught me over the years. In the first place I came
to realize that even Marxists cannot interpret a literary text till
they have understood it exactly and know what the author was
trying to express and what he managed to convey. Another
thing I learnt both from literary history and from acquaintances
with authors of our own day was that any artist's exposition of
his own work can play an interesting and essential part in its
critical interpretation, but that the critic must not place too
much reliance on it. What Thomas Mann aimed to convey in
The Magic Mountain and what the modern critic finds on reading

it are two different things. Furthermore, I believe any kind of criticism to be basically dishonest which does not set out to make the critic's own person and position in the world an integral part of the analysis. Criticism is inconceivable without some conscious representation of the historical relationship between the critic in his time and the author in his. And finally—this is where the contrast with T. S. Eliot again emerges—when considering a work of literature I cannot separate the question of function from that of substance. What that means Dr. Steiner has already explained in his essay. That is my opinion too.

Thus the contemporary writers and works that most interest me are those where I am conscious of a definite attempt to knit function and substance together. And so I would answer the Editor's query about what modern works interest me by saying that since Brecht's death I have looked forward to any new works by Friedrich Dürrenmatt with impatience, that any new book by Sartre is bound to interest me, that I am agog to read the new Günter Grass novel which is due this autumn and am keenly awaiting fresh plays by such English dramatists as Pinter and Wesker. Does this seem rather an eclectic programme, or is there a critical and also an ethical attitude behind it? I hope it is more than mere eclecticism.

EMILIO CECCHI

Is Empiricism Too Parochial?

━━━━━━━━━ ◆◌◌◌◆ ━━━━━━━━━

I think that the best way of saving space and of achieving clarity is to answer first of all your five questions and then to append some short general remarks. So here I come to your first question: English and American critics had an influence on my formation and my development. My contact with them came about all the more necessarily owing to the fact that, during my twenties, I was already interesting myself in English and American literature. I was then translating Shelley's *A Defence of Poetry*, and it was easy for me to observe how certain ideas of G. B. Vico (on which, by way of German philosophy, the *Defence* is partly based) had acquired a new vitality in Benedetto Croce's aesthetic, which was then beginning to make itself heard.

While studying the early romantics of England, it was natural to make acquaintance with Coleridge. In respect of the importance to be attributed to Coleridge's critical work, not less than to his poetry, I was encouraged by the support given to me by C. H. Herford of Manchester University in his article in the *Manchester Guardian* (July 4, 1919) on a book which I had then published, and which has lately been reprinted under the title *I grandi romantici inglesi* (Sansoni: Florence). In Italy the critical course which I was trying to pursue had its foundations in Vico, De Sanctis and Croce. But none of what I successively learnt from a quantity of other critics of literature and figurative art conflicted with that course. Of these, among the English there were Walter Pater and the so-called 'decadents' right on

116

to Ernest de Selincourt, Kenneth Clark and Virginia Woolf; among the Americans, from Poe onwards, they include Matthiessen, Berenson and Edmund Wilson.

There is no conflict between that critical attitude of mine, essentially dependent upon that of Vico and Croce, and the study of other critics who derive from different strains. Croce, for instance, was always considered a systematic and extremely rigorous thinker and critic; yet he admired a book such as *The Italian Painters of the Renaissance* by that highly gifted empiricist, Berenson, and went so far as to compare it with De Sanctis's *Storia della Litteratura Italiana*. And, though he was the bitter enemy of all aestheticism and decadentism, he wrote more than thirty years ago in his *Aesthetica in nuce* (1928) these striking words:

'In the second half of the nineteenth century all that was best in thought about art is not to be found in the work of philosophers or professional writers on aesthetics, but in that of the critics of art and poetry, such as De Sanctis in Italy, Baudelaire and Flaubert in France, Pater in England, Hanslick and Fiedler in Germany. Only these men really console us for the aesthetic trivialities of the positivist philosophers and the laboured vacuities of the so-called idealists. . . .'

Your second question induces me to enter into fuller details as to my contacts with English and American criticism to which I have already alluded. I was particularly impressed by the concrete tone and urbane handling of the English, by their refusal to yield to the temptation to rhetoric, to adopt complicated speculative apparatus, and to take up too ponderous didactic attitudes. I was won over by their preference for approaching the *common reader*, as Virginia Woolf would have said, by their subtle use of *understatement* and a secret *flavour* of irony which, all the same, hardly ever diminishes the lively sense of mutual human intercourse. English criticism is not invariably or without exception adorned with these virtues; but I have always been able to imbibe from it ample satisfaction and profit.

I must add that the tradition of the *essay*, so strong in England, is not just limited to the fanciful and imaginative forms created and perfected by Addison, Lamb, Stevenson, Beerbohm and Virginia Woolf. Some of its intimate energy and its grace was naturally bound to flow into essays on critical and literary subjects, or at least into the best examples of them. Certainly the admirable grace of style and the bright lucidity of the best English criticism have not only a formal and ornamental value but they are an integral part of it and inseparable from its ideological substance, in fact from its truth.

In connexion with all this, I do not consider that the *Anglo-Saxon attitude* in the discussion of literature and art can differ intrinsically from that which is represented by the criticism based on other traditions of culture. From art and literature people ask but one thing, which is always the same and always new. It cannot be otherwise. If it were, we should find no importance in the *Agamemnon*, in the *Georgics*, in the Parthenon and in ancient Chinese painting: but we do find them highly important. And, to give another example, the treatise on *The Sublime* is as lively to us as though it was written only yesterday.

In many cases, what seem to be different, or hitherto quite undiscovered, principles of criticism, are no more than criteria of meaning or value assumed for the framing of aesthetic judgments, though in fact they have nothing to do with aesthetics. Sometimes, it is true, they do reflect genuine stimuli and new vital impulses present in the social, political, or any other reality of the modern world. But their true place is in the field of action. When they are brought in and applied in the house of aesthetics and of criticism, artistic and literary—that is to say, in the contemplative field—they are nothing but errors.

Let us leave out of account the old, ingenuous moralistic and puritanical intransigences; but today, particularly, one could point out a whole range of these applications of arbitrary principles, which for the most part have a clear basis of pragmatism. There is the Marxist fatalism and propagandism; and, while worthy in and for itself of great interest, there is Freudian 'scientism'. Then, there is a real *tarantula* in the superstition and mania of 'avant-gardism at all costs'. This is related to the other superstition of 'experimentalism', from which, by the application of appropriate formulas (e.g., the *école du regard*), we were to expect decisive innovations in the novel, in lyric poetry and in the drama—novelties which can only arise from an individual inspiration. Finally there are the numerous varieties and combinations, sincere and insincere, of existentialist disquiet.

In spite of this it seems to me that in the course of time, the object of criticism is and remains simpler and more constant than might appear from the changes and the clashes of forms and methods, and from the diversity of cultural traditions. If we try, for instance, to place De Sanctis in the picture of the criticism of his day, in two different traditions, such as the French and the Anglo-Saxon, his nearest neighbours are Sainte-Beuve and Pater. (And it is surprising that recently Professor Wellek has preferred to put Taine rather than Sainte-Beuve by his side, by reason of their common Hegelian descent, but the truth is that De Sanctis, even at his roughest and most immature, never allowed this descent to lead him, as it led Taine, into completely mechanical and aprioristic applications of Hegelian theory.)

In De Sanctis, of course, there are no hints of any affinity with Sainte-Beuve's love of psychological and biographical detail; nor are there any traces of that melancholy, Alexandrian, rather sickly mysticism of the Beautiful—with a capital B—that one finds in Pater, of whose name, too, De Sanctis can never have heard. But this is less important than the fact that these three great and fundamental nineteenth-century critics shared one essential gift to a degree which perhaps has never subsequently been reached. That is the gift of identifying the vital centre of a personality and of a work of art, by bringing the reader before it, not so much by dint of analysis, proof, documentation and other expository methods, but with a revelatory vividness in which aesthetic emotion and historical judgment are perfectly fused.

Rather than trying to formulate theoretically the principles of a critical attitude based on all that I learned from the models whom I have mentioned I was more interested in attempting to put these principles into the best concrete forms of which my abilities were capable. Changes of direction did not seem to me necessary, but rather integration and enrichment. Among these attempts were my studies of the history of art, taking Berenson as my master, especially as regards that second flowering of European figurative genius which, after the golden age of Greece, was the Italian Renaissance, though today so many critics, whom it is superfluous to mention, affect to deny the values of the Renaissance as much as possible.

But, if my work was not an evolution or a replacement of these principles and tendencies by others, I think it is possible to recognize in it a continuous effort to achieve an always greater lucidity and precision of statement. I have already said that, in my opinion, the style of a critical essay is a guarantee of the truth and vitality of the impressions and ideas set forth in it, and in fact is an intrinsic part of that truth and vitality.

What is asked of poetry, art and literature? One can only repeat that old answer—always the same—which, anyhow, satisfied Goethe and Tolstoy: from poetry and literature one asks the truth. It is not an empirical but a transcendental truth, enclosed in a form that bears all the marks of time, but is valid above and beyond time, and preserves all the highest significances of human experience. As for the fifth and last of your questions, asking in what authors and works, of any age or country, this truth is most loftily expressed, I should have to reply with a far too long and cumbrous autobiographical book which it is luckily impossible to write here. I confine myself to naming some foreign writers who have lived in our day—Proust, Mann, Musil, Kafka, Virginia Woolf, Joyce, Valéry, Eliot. . . . One must admit that if, since the beginning of the century, we have abundantly suffered the doom of wars, dictatorships and revolutions, etc., it has also been good to follow out life's journey during a time when those authors were producing such works.

As for *The Times Literary Supplement* of July 26, 1963, one matter certainly did not escape the notice of those who put it together, but on the contrary they devoted to it a kind of 'warning' or editorial 'justification'. Among other things they had rightly observed that 'literary critics of the first order are rarer than first order writers of any other sort'. And this is re-echoed by another aphorism on the same page: 'the critic as primarily a man of letters has become almost an extinct animal'. All this was gracefully expressed, but perhaps not without a certain ambiguity, considering that critical and literary personalities of the stature of Benedetto Croce, of a Thomas Mann, and also (let me add) of an Ortega y Gasset, though a lesser one, are creatures hardly even of yesterday.

The fact is that, starting with this kind of bias, and also as a consequence of the undeniable decadence of so-called 'journalistic' criticism, the recruiting of those who contributed to this *Supplement* was restricted, in the end, almost exclusively to the Anglo-American university world. In its pages not only did one look in vain for contributions from an Edmund Wilson, an Eliot, a Kazin, and from lesser but already authoritative writers; but similarly in the various articles by René Wellek, L. C. Knights, George Steiner, Richard Hoggart, W. W. Robson, John Wain, Harry Levin, Graham Hough, etc., one must say there was hardly a trace of any substantial constructive reference, not only to Wilson, Eliot and other contemporaries of ours, but to masters of yesterday such as Croce and Mann, not to speak of masters of the day before yesterday, now more alive than ever, such as Sainte-Beuve, Pater and De Sanctis.

When reading many pages of these donnish articles one had the impression of struggling with difficulty through the narrows of a characteristic and clever empiricism and particularism that might almost be called parochial. British insularity is attractive in many aspects and for many reasons: but, if it had needed to justify itself in the field of debate on matters so universal as these, it could hardly have chosen better advocates than these so subtle, intricate and thorny pages. An exception was made to this sense of isolation by the generous reference to the great Coleridge in Professor Knights's article: but in the diffuse and almost stock phrases referring to Matthew Arnold there was only a vague jumbling together of his puritan moralism and his pagan neoclassicism, both indeed respectable, but now rather cold and unserviceable.

Altogether, it seemed to me to stand out very plainly that, in Anglo-Saxon culture, the gulf between what we may call free 'journalistic' criticism and the academic, donnish criticism, closely and professionally bound to a didactic function, must be deeper and more unsurmountable than it is in Latin Europe. From this point of view the open-mindedness of Croce seems all the more admirable when, thirty years ago, he wrote such words as I have already quoted above from his *Aesthetica in nuce*.

I consider that in the present disorder and want of direction in criticism, which is the prerogative of no one country but afflicts them all, one of the most desirable and urgent things would be the achievement everywhere of an ever closer bond of relationship and mutual accommodation between the academic world of the universities and that of the free or 'journalistic' critics. Their reciprocal stand-offishness and suspiciousness are damaging to both of them, and above all to the reader. The misunderstanding and strained relations which at one time occurred between Carducci and De Sanctis and their respective followers were very nearly repeating themselves when Croce's *Aestetica* appeared: and Croce's conquest of the universities came about less through professorial agency than through that of free criticism and of the organs of public opinion. Therefore I ascribe a great usefulness to 'symposiums' like this one of *The Times Literary Supplement*, in which inquiries and discussions on situations and opinions can be carried on with absolute frankness, even though, for my part, I am afraid—and I apologize—that I have expressed points of view that may need to be corrected.

ROLAND BARTHES

Criticism as Language

———————◆⤲◦⤳◆———————

I t is always possible to promulgate certain major critical principles in the light of contemporary ideology, especially in
France, where theoretical formulations carry great weight, no
doubt because they give the practising critic the assurance that
he is, at one and the same time, taking part in a fight, making
history and exemplifying a philosophical system. We can say
that, during the last fifteen years French criticism has developed, with various degrees of success, with four great 'philo-
sophies'. There is, first of all, Existentialism, or what is
generally so called, although the appropriateness of the term is
debatable; it has produced Sartre's critical works, his studies of
Baudelaire and Flaubert, his shorter articles on Proust, Mauriac,
Giraudoux and Ponge, and above all his outstanding book on
Genet. Next Marxism; it is well known by now (the matter was
thrashed out long ago) that orthodox Marxism has proved
critically sterile through offering a purely mechanical explanation of works of literature and providing slogans rather than
criteria of value. It follows that the most fruitful criticism has to
be looked for, as it were, on the frontiers of Marxism, not at its
recognized centre. The work of Lucien Goldmann on Racine,
Pascal, the 'New Novel', the avant-garde theatre and Malraux
owes a large and explicit debt to Lukács, and it would be difficult to imagine a more flexible and ingenious form of criticism
based on political and social history. Then there is psycho-
analysis; at the moment, the best representative of Freudian
psycho-analytical criticism is Charles Mauron, who has written

on Racine and Mallarmé. But here again, 'marginal' activities have proved more fruitful. Gaston Bachelard, starting from an analysis of substances rather than of works and tracing the dynamic distortions of imagery in a great many poets, founded a whole critical school which is, indeed, so prolific that present-day French criticism in its most flourishing aspect can be said to be Bachelardian in inspiration (G. Poulet, J. Starobinski, J.-P. Richard), Lastly, there is structuralism (which, if reduced to extremely simple, perhaps excessively simple, terms, might be called formalism); the movement has been important, one might almost say fashionable, in France since Claude Lévi-Strauss brought it into the social sciences and philosophical reflection. So far, it has produced very few critical works, but such works are in preparation and they will no doubt show the influence of the linguistic model worked out by de Saussure and elaborated by Roman Jakobson (who, in his earlier years, belonged to a literary critical movement, the Russian formalist school). It would seem possible, for instance, to develop a variety of literary criticism on the basis of the two rhetorical categories established by Jakobson, metaphor and metonymy.

As can be seen, this French criticism is both 'national' (it owes little or nothing to Anglo-American, Spitzerian or Crocian criticism) and up to date or—if the expression seems preferable —'unfaithful to the past' (since it belongs entirely to an aspect of contemporary ideology, it can hardly consider itself as being indebted to any critical tradition, whether founded by Sainte-Beuve, Taine or Lanson). However, the last-named type of criticism raises a particular problem in this connexion. Lanson was the prototype of the French teacher of literature and, during the last fifty years, his work, method and mentality, as transmitted by innumerable disciples, have continued to govern academic criticism. Since the principles, or at least the declared principles, of this kind of criticism are accuracy and objectivity in the establishment of facts, it might be thought that there would be no incompatibility between Lansonianism and the various forms of ideological criticism, which are all interpreta-

tive. But although most present-day French critics (I am thinking of those who deal with structure, not those concerned with
current reviewing) are themselves teachers, there is a certain
amount of tension between interpretative and positivistic (academic) criticism. The reason is that Lansonianism is itself an
ideology; it is not simply content to demand the application of
the objective rules of all scientific research, it also implies certain general convictions about man, history, literature and the
relationship between the author and his work. For instance,
Lansonian psychology is quite out of date, since it consists
fundamentally of a kind of analogical determinism, according
to which the details of a given work must resemble the details
of the author's life, the characters the innermost being of the
author, and so on. This makes it a very peculiar ideology because, since it was invented, psychology has, among other things,
imagined the opposite relationship of negation between the
work and the author. Of course, it is inevitable that an ideology
should be based on philosophical postulates; the argument
against Lansonianism is not that it has assumptions, but that
instead of admitting them, it drapes them in a moral cloak of
rigorous and objective investigation; it is as if ideology were
being smuggled surreptitiously into the scientific approach.

Since these different ideological principles can coexist *simultaneously* (and for my part, I can, in a certain sense, accept both
simultaneously), we have to conclude that the ideological choice
is not the essence of criticism nor 'truth' its ultimate test.
Criticism is something other than making correct statements in
the light of 'true' principles. It follows that the major sin in
criticism is not to have an ideology but to keep quiet about it.
There is a name for this kind of guilty silence; it is self-deception or bad faith. How can anyone believe that a given work is
an *object* independent of the psyche and personal history of the
critic studying it, with regards to which he enjoys a sort of
extraterritorial status? It would be a very remarkable thing if
the profound relationship that most critics postulate between the
author they are dealing with and his works were non-existent in

the case of their own works and their own situation in time. It is inconceivable that the creative laws governing the writer should not also be valid for the critic. All criticism must include (although it may do so in the most indirect and discreet way) an implicit comment on itself; all criticism is criticism both of the work under consideration and of the critic; to quote Claudel's pun, it is knowledge (connaissance) of the other and co-birth (co-naissance) of oneself to the world. Or, to express the same thing in still another way, criticism is not in any sense a table of results or a body of judgments; it is essentially an activity, that is to say a series of intellectual acts inextricably involved with the historical and subjective (the two terms are synonymous) existence of the person who carries them out and has to assume responsibility for them. It is pointless to ask whether or not an activity is 'true'; the imperatives governing it are quite different.

Whatever the complexities of literary theory, a novelist or a poet is supposed to speak about objects and phenomena which, whether imaginary or not, are external and anterior to language. The world exists and the writer uses language; such is the definition of literature. The object of criticism is very different; it deals not with 'the world', but with the linguistic formulations made by others; it is a comment on a comment, a secondary language or *meta*-language (as the logicians would say), applied to a primary language (or language-as-object). It follows that critical activity must take two kinds of relationships into account: the relationship between the critical language and the language of the author under consideration and the relationship between the latter (language-as-object) and the world. Criticism is defined by the interaction of these two languages and so bears a close resemblance to another intellectual activity, logic, which is also entirely founded on the distinction between language-as-object and meta-language.

Consequently, if criticism is only a meta-language, its task is not to discover forms of 'truth' but forms of 'validity'. In itself, a language cannot be true or false; it is either valid or non-valid.

It is valid when it consists of a coherent system of signs. The rules governing the language of literature are not concerned with the correspondence between that language and reality (whatever the claims made by schools of realism), but only with its being in line with the system of signs that the author has decided on (of course, in this connexion great stress must be laid on the term *system*). It is not the business of criticism to decide whether Proust told 'the truth'—whether, for instance, Baron de Charlus was really Montesquiou or Françoise, Céleste or even, more generally, whether the society Proust describes is an adequate representation of the historical conditions in which the aristocracy was finally eliminated at the end of the nineteenth century—its function is purely to evolve its own language and to make it as coherent and logical, that is as systematic, as possible, so that it can render an account of, or better still 'integrate' (in the mathematical sense) the greatest possible quantity of Proust's language just as a logical equation tests the validity of a piece of reasoning, without taking sides about the 'truth' of the arguments used. We might say that the task of criticism (and this is the only guarantee of its universality) is purely formal; it does not consist in 'discovering' in the work or the author under consideration something 'hidden' or 'profound' or 'secret' which has so far escaped notice (through what miracle? Are we more perceptive than our predecessors?) but only in *fitting together*—as a skilled cabinet maker, by a process of 'intelligent' fumbling, interlocks two parts of a complicated piece of furniture—the language of the day (Existentialism, Marxism or psychoanalysis) and the language of the author, that is, the formal system of logical rules that he evolved in the conditions of his time. The 'proof' of a given form of criticism is not 'alethiological' in nature (i.e., is not concerned with the truth), since critical writing, like logical writing, can never be other than tautology; in the last resort, it consists in the delayed statement (but the delay, through being fully accepted, is itself significant) that 'Racine is Racine', 'Proust is Proust'. If there is such a thing as a critical proof, it lies not in the ability to *discover* the work under consideration but, on the contrary, to *cover* it as completely as possible with one's own language.

In this respect too, then, criticism is an essentially formal activity, not in the aesthetic, but in the logical sense of the term. It might be said that the only means by which criticism can avoid the self-deception or bad faith referred to earlier is to set itself the moral aim not of deciphering the meaning of the work under consideration, but of reconstituting the rules and compulsions which governed the elaboration of that sense; provided always it is also agreed that a work of literature is a very special semantic system, the aim of which is to put 'meaning' into the world, but not 'a meaning'. A work of literature, at least of the kind that is normally considered by the critics (and this itself may be a possible definition of 'good' literature) is neither ever quite meaningless (mysterious or 'inspired') nor ever quite clear; it is, so to speak, *suspended* meaning; it offers itself to the reader as a declared system of significance, but as a signified object it eludes his grasp. This kind of *dis-appointment* or *deception* (de-capio: un-take) inherent in the meaning explains how it is that a work of literature has such power to ask questions of the world (by undermining the definite meanings that seem to be the apanage of beliefs, ideologies and common sense) without, however, supplying any answers (no great work is 'dogmatic'): it also explains how a work can go on being reinterpreted indefinitely, since there is no reason why critics should ever stop discussing Racine or Shakespeare (except through an act of abandonment which would itself be a kind of language). Literature, since it consists at one and the same time of the insistent offering of a meaning and the persistent elusiveness of that meaning, is definitely no more than a language, that is, a system of signs; its being lies not in the message but in the system. This being so, the critic is not called upon to reconstitute the message of the work, but only its system, just as the business of the linguist is not to decipher the meaning of a sentence but to determine the formal structure which permits the transmission of its meaning.

CRITICISM AS LANGUAGE

It is precisely through the admission, on the part of criticism, that it is only a language (or, more accurately, a meta-language) that it can, paradoxically yet genuinely, be objective and subjective, historical and existential, totalitarian and liberal. The language that a critic chooses to speak is not a gift from heaven; it is one of the range of languages offered by his situation in time and, objectively, it is the latest stage of a certain historical development of knowledge, ideas and intellectual passions; it is a *necessity*. On the other hand, each critic chooses this necessary language, in accordance with a certain existential pattern, as the *means of exercising* an intellectual function which is his, and his alone, putting into the operation his 'deepest self', that is, his preferences, pleasures, resistances and obsessions. In this way the critical work contains within itself a dialogue between two historical situations and two subjectivities, those of the author and those of the critic. But this dialogue shows a complete egotistical bias towards the present; criticism is neither a 'tribute' to the truth of the past nor to the truth of 'the other'; it is the ordering of that which is intelligible in our own time.

EMIL STAIGER

Time and the Poetic Imagination

───────────◆⇌◦⇌◆───────────

The method of literary criticism to which I still subscribe was first put forward in 1939 in my book *Die Zeit als Einbildungskraft des Dichters*. There it was argued in the introduction that 'We must grasp what grips us'; that is, not something that lies behind or beneath the poetry, not an abstract idea, not any psychological backgrounds, or social preconditions, but quite directly the artistic content, the poetic element, or, if you like, the 'beautiful'. This concept of beauty however is liable to misunderstanding. Anybody who demands beauty of the work of art arouses the suspicion that he is bound to a Classical ideal. The answer to this is that beauty here means no more nor less than 'unity in complexity'. In this sense a novel by Dostoevsky is no less beautiful than a tragedy of Sophocles, a horrible nightmare by Kafka no less than Pope's 'Rape of the Lock'. The many various aspects—image, motif, idea, choice of words, syntax, metre, and whatever else one might add—harmonize, and present themselves as an indivisible unity. And it is just this harmony that makes the work of art 'beautiful' or artistically perfect.

What makes for a harmonious work of art? What is it that comes across as the unity of complexity? It is what we call 'style'. This concept, too, requires explanation. What makes a poem like Goethe's 'Wanderers Nachtlied' a work of art is not simply its motif, evening in a central German landscape, nor is it the way we feel our own inner tranquillity confirmed by the tranquillity settling on the mountains. All this could be said in unpoetical prose. Nor is it the stanza per se, the succession of unaccented and accented syllables or the simple sentence construction. One could imagine this same stanza employed for other motifs where it would not be appropriate. There are poems in which the form conflicts awkwardly with the content. 'Wanderers Nachtlied' is beautiful only because it is a harmonious whole.

But what can this unity be, if it is neither image, nor the comparison of the inner and outer realms, nor the stanza, nor any other single aspect? We sense it distinctly but it is not easy to name. And it is no coincidence that this should present difficulties.

The unprejudiced reader will say that the whole poem is unambiguously informed by Goethe's individuality. We agree without hesitation, but the question is: what is meant by individuality? It would appear to be up to psychology to give the answer. But psychology separates individuality into characteristics, or it refers us to the unconscious and subconscious, to drives, attitudes and things of that nature. This approach distracts from the unity which was so clearly felt in the beautiful work of art.

We can learn more from Gustav Becking's book, *Der musikalische Rhythmus als Erkenntnisquelle* (1928, second edition 1958). This author asks us to take a baton while listening to music, and to beat time with complete freedom. A test will show that the beat varies from Mozart to Bach and Handel, and again from Wagner to Schumann. The figure which we describe as we beat time may be reduced to a diagram on paper. Becking calls this the *Schlagfigur*, and he refers to its meaning as the 'rhythm'. In the *Schlagfiguren*, which vary greatly in size, shape and tendency, we see the 'rhythm', and there, according to Becking, we have the individual uniqueness of the composer expressed in a hieroglyphic. In this sense the 'rhythm' is apparently what uniformly pulses through and informs a sustained composition. It is the audible or, in the hieroglyphic, the visible style, the stamp of individuality which has been impressed upon all the separate parts.

Basically this method may also be applied to literature, and the analysis of sounds by Sievers, Rutz and Nohl may be mentioned as experiments. But verse or even prose sentences cannot guide the hand executing the *Schlagfigur* so surely as music, which sweeps us along irresistibly. And anyway, what is the advantage of reducing a poem to a *Schlagfigur*? How shall we find our way back to its multiplicity, which still needs to be developed out of its unity?

Here we are helped by Martin Heidegger's *Sein und Zeit* (1927) and *Vom Wesen des Grundes* (1931). It may seem at first as though we were passing to a completely different topic, but the connexion with Becking's 'rhythm' will become clear soon enough. Naturally it is not our purpose here to come to terms with the whole of Heidegger's philosophical achievement. I shall only indicate how far it has become important for my work.

The 'time' mentioned in the title of Heidegger's book is not the objective time of clock or calendar. What is meant rather, is time as 'inner meaning', as a 'form of contemplation' in the sense previously elaborated by Kant, who, however, was confining himself to the demands of the exact sciences. For Heidegger 'time' is the essential ingredient of all reality. The fact that my world is different from the world of a person of antiquity or of the Middle Ages, and that the world of a hero is not the same as that of the ordinary man in the street, rests on the differing part played by 'time' as 'inner meaning'. How far do I take account of the future in present-day affairs; how far can I plan and project? In this the Christian, who accepts the redemptionist view of history known in German as *Heilsgeschichte*, will clearly act differently from the Greek, who lives in a more visualized present. What meaning must be given to the past? Similarly a German Romantic doubtless thinks and feels differently from Schiller, who fixes his gaze on lofty, unattainable goals.

Heidegger, it is true, would scarcely be interested in such conclusions from his teaching. More concerned with this problem are E. Minkowski's book, *Le temps vécu* (1933), and Ludwig Binswanger's *Grundformen und Erkenntnis menschlichen Daseins* (1942) or George Poulet's *Études sur le temps humain* (1949). All these are about the existence of man, understood in its core as 'time'—just the same subject, in fact, as was covered in 1939 in the field of literary criticism by a title that at first put the public off, but is none the less exact: *Die Zeit als Einbildungskraft des Dichters.* 'Time as the Force of the Writer's Imagination.'

The interaction of planning, commemoration, and the impulse of the moment, of profound memory, power of expectation and the formation of a present more or less affected by past and future, and accordingly more or less deprived or sated—this whole interplay which varies with times, peoples and individuals, and is inexhaustible in its possibilities—this we understand best perhaps as a basic form of movement of the human spirit, as inner tension and gravitation. And with this we are reminded of the *Schlagfiguren*, of 'rhythm' as understood by Becking. The *Schlagfigur* is an image, a hieroglyph representing 'time' as the force of the imagination. 'Time' as the force of the imagination and rhythm in Becking's sense are the same thing. It is rhythm, it is 'time' as inner gravitation and tension, which is the underlying unity sustaining the complexity of the work of art.

Various problems arise at this point, but it is impossible to deal with them in detail. There is for instance the question of how we are to regard ugliness, lack of beauty, ordinary dull banality, if man's being is founded in 'time' as the force of the imagination. All I can say is that in so far as a uniform rhythm comes across in a work we call it beautiful or artistically perfect.

I now at last turn to the process of interpretation. When I interpret poetry I have to begin by clearly grasping the all-pervading rhythm and trying to re-create it within myself. That is, I am concerned with what since Herder has been called *Einfühlung.* This kind of empathy requires the interpretative critic to be artistically gifted. Unlike most people today I am convinced that without such gifts nothing of consequence can be achieved in the field of literary criticism. Anyone who cannot feel empathetically and obey the rhythm of the work will go astray again and again and will do violence to the work of art.

This quiet, selfless empathy, however, is only the first step. Any critic aiming to make a more reliable statement than the gifted layman must try to see the rhythm clearly as an individual modification of 'time', of the inner meaning. In this task he will get some help from the poets' meditations on the subject of time. Goethe, for instance, saw time as he understood it as a moment (*Augenblick*), that moment of the present where the past is still with us and the future already alive:

> *Dann ist Vergangenheit beständig,*
> *Das Künftige voraus lebendig,*
> *Der Aügenblick ist Ewigkeit*
> GOETHE: 'Vermächtnis'

Ludwig Tieck provides a suggestive idea in the 'reversible time' of his comedy, *Die verkehrte Welt*. But even where such indications are lacking it must be fundamentally possible to understand rhythm as the rule of 'time'. Clemens Brentano, for one, probably never reflected upon time as such. Nevertheless, it is easy to see that his 'time' is a fleeting shuffle from one moment to the next.

The next task is to show how time fulfils itself in the complexity of one work of art. All three volumes of my *Goethe* (1952–9), for example, are concerned solely with the 'moment', which is demonstrated not only in *Faust*, where it is a key word in the pact with Mephistopheles, but also in the organic composition of *Hermann und Dorothea*, in the drunken hymns of youth, in the wisdom of the *West-östlicher Divan*, in the writings on the natural sciences, even in the conduct of Goethe's own life. Everywhere, though in different ways at different times in his career, one finds the present when the past is still with us and the future already alive; and the equilibrium so typical of this writer is thereby achieved.

Any mistakes underlying one's approach to the interpretation correct themselves sooner or later, so long as the subject does not have to be given up as inaccessible. For everything must harmonize with everything else. Any disharmony accordingly demands immediate revision. When finally the unity of the complexity is demonstrated or the complexity developed from an all-determining rhythm, the interpretation acquires a validity which is unprovable, perhaps, but does not require proof. It is not even necessary to put into words the part played by 'time' as the force of the imagination as we ourselves have come to realize it. On the contrary, it is advisable to remove the abstract scaffolding once it has served its purpose. The unity once comprehended will not again be lost in the complexity. It consolidates the interpretation.

Admittedly many of the countless interpretations which have appeared in the last few decades lack this firmness in temporal structure. They make do with putting forward an agreeable paraphrase of the contents and a few vague notes about the beauty of the language. This is where literary criticism becomes amateurish.

Nor is there any more to be said for the view that it is enough simply to formulate one's first impressions, in other words to do no more than describe a subjective experience. Anybody who concerns himself more or less seriously with the past knows how difficult it is to understand even the plain text as the author meant it, and how exact one's knowledge of living conditions and of cultural and political circumstances must be if the attempted empathy is not to be replaced by pure caprice. This means that any adequate interpretation has to be based on thorough historical study. The better I know a period to which a poem belongs, the less likely I am to go astray. It is for this and no other reason that my books deal exclusively with German literature. I cannot trust my ear to hear English and French verse accurately enough to be absolutely sure of their rhythm, the 'time' which unifies their complexity.

Lastly, the question of evaluation. American criticism in particular, more recently followed to an increasing extent by German literary criticism too, requires the critic to pass an objectively valid judgment on the rank and value of the work of art, and for this reason finds fault with the method of interpretation described here, which does nothing of the sort and leaves its readers to judge for themselves. To this it should be said that in so far as the beauty of a work is grounded in the harmony of the parts, interpretation too deals with evaluation. It will show, for example, that Goethe's 'Mailied' falls back into the anacreontic style in its conclusion, or that in *Emilia Galotti* Lessing fails to follow the catastrophe to its logical conclusion, obviously for political reasons. Who will deny that such faults detract from the value of the work of art? The question becomes more difficult when it is a matter of comparing flawless works of different styles, such as Classical and Romantic. Of course, no one can stop the interpretative critic giving vent to his personal beliefs. But can such beliefs be substantiated by valid criteria? And is this even desirable? Any evaluation that does more than show the harmony of the parts says something about the critic, but scarcely about the work of art. This is as it should be, for a truly objectively valid scale of values would be dangerous for the creative artist and would destroy the reader's enjoyment of the changeable history of the human spirit. Nevertheless, *one* consideration would perhaps be justified. It could be asked which style is best suited to the nature of language. Certain Romantic poems like the hymns of Novalis seem very tenuous and threaten to vanish altogether at the lightest touch. Protestant poetry of the Baroque period tends to be too rigid. The twentieth-century psychological novel loses its way among the subtleties of the lonely soul, which in the end defy communication. Thus various paths obviously lead beyond the boundaries of language. Other writers meanwhile remain more in the centre of their medium. Once again, nobody can be prevented from cheerfully applauding poetry's disintegration by means of poetry. But whoever believes in poetry as such will prefer poets who maintain a balance between extremes and take a vital and creative middle road. In this way—and with this decisive reservation—a scale of values could be established. In my opinion, however, it is better to do without, and to allow the creative instinct its head.

In all this I have consciously limited myself to *one* aspect of my work, to the 'art of interpretation'. My book with this title (*Die Kunst der Interpretation*) appeared in 1955 and rests entirely upon the earlier work *Die Zeit als Einbildungskraft des Dichters. Grundbegriffe der Poetik* (Fundamentals of Poetics, 1946) has a completely different end in view. It sets out to show that lyric, epos and drama in the form of poem, verse narration and stage play have to be distinguished from lyrical, epic and dramatic as such. The latter are names for stylistic elements that are operative in every kind of poetry, regardless of outer form. How far this division into lyric, epic and dramatic quality is once again rooted in 'time', time as the power of the writer's imagination; how the linguistic elements of syllable, word and sentence are mirrored in it, how this approach is related to Ernst Cassirer's *Philosophie der symbolischen Formen* (Vol. 1, 1923): all these are questions which cannot be dealt with here. Probably there would be little point if they were. For my book has consistently been misunderstood as a prescriptive poetics, in spite of all warnings to the contrary. Actually its place is less with literary criticism than with philosophical anthropology in its widest sense.

Finally, the book *Stilwandel* (1963) represents an attempt not to derive the movements and changes in literary history from any outer causes, but instead to grasp all human activity as a stylistic phenomenon and so to explain changes of styles purely in terms of the prevailing stylistic situation.

UMBERTO ECO

The Analysis of Structure

———————————— ❖◦❖ ————————————

Before I define my indebtedness to Anglo-American criticism, there are one or two points I ought to make clear. I am not a critic in the normal sense of the word; academically speaking I rank as a philosopher, and my concern is aesthetics. I am particularly interested in the history of poetics; I feel, indeed, that today more than ever aesthetics ought to start with a phenomenology of the various notions of art prevalent among artists and artistic movements of different countries and periods. Students of poetics are often unable to refer to any explicit documents and have to establish the poetics implicit in any creative artist's achievement by examining the structure of his works and identifying the aims of his whole activity; in this way research into poetics becomes tantamount to a concrete analysis of the works. The point is not to draw a distinction between their ugly and their beautiful aspects so as to establish which parts of them are valid, but to describe *structural models*. It is in this sense that the examination of poetics can be held to be a kind of critical activity, and its results used as a contribution to the critical understanding of a particular work or writer. At present, poetics are coming more and more to get the upper hand of the work of art—starting from the 'poetry about poetry' of romantic and decadent tradition, we have now moved on to complex works which seem virtually to identify with their own theorizing; think of *Finnegans Wake*, for instance. So the question now arises, however paradoxically and hypothetically, whether we are not fast approaching the moment when research into poetics will be the only possible form of criticism.

My second point is that having made a lengthy study of James Joyce (to whom I devoted half my last book, *Opera Aperta*) I could easily base an account of my relationship with Anglo-American criticism on my own interests, for in my case it was natural to refer to authors like Levin, Wilson, Gilbert, Tindall, Beckett, Pound and Eliot, to name only a few of them. But when I look back to my formative years I begin to wonder whether it was Joyce who led me to these critics, or the reading of them and of Anglo-American criticism in general that led me to Joyce.

I am of course speaking of my own formation and I am not putting myself forward as a typical case; but I think I can say that a similar interest in Anglo-American criticism is common to many of my generation. My tastes were formed in the postwar years; in a period, that is, when many young Italian intellectuals reacted against the virtual cultural dictatorship of Croce. By this I do not of course mean to refer to the role which Croce's philosophy played in spreading ideas of freedom under Fascism; I mean that there was a philosophical-cum-critical attempt to rescue and develop certain seeds of opposition to idealism which isolated groups had been scattering in the course of the previous fifty years: from existentialism to Christian personalism, from pragmatism to neo-positivism and Marxism.

It was this that compelled us to establish contact, fired by an often exaggerated but none the less understandable *vis polemica*, with the schools of thought that idealism disapproved of. And many of us found that the Anglo-American cultural sphere provided fertile ground for exploration, just as the generations before ours had found with the German. I am thinking particularly of Dewey on the one hand, and also of the various neo-positivist trends and the schools of linguistic analysis; at the same time there was the new consideration of sociological methods—often applied to the interpretation of artistic phenomena (not least thanks to the influence of Marxism, as this encouraged the establishment of closer links between cultural, social and economic phenomena).

It was essentially a way of applying stricter empirical tests and a more precise terminology to cultural attitudes and habits of thought derived from idealism and its influence. And if many of us felt that the operation had succeeded this did not mean that all Croce's teachings had to be rejected *en bloc*. I think that in our way of thinking and of looking at problems, even if this took place in the light of the new methodology, certain principles remained as permanent elements characterizing our researches. But let me move on to a concrete instance, and look at the aesthetic problem.

There remains something 'Crocian' in my own attitude, for instance, in my conviction that even when an artistic 'genre' like the novel is under concrete discussion the ultimate aim of aesthetics is still to set up categories capable of explaining the phenomenon of art as such. Except that I see this as the final stage (and am willing to admit the possibility of failure); before which I would put concrete research work on facts which Croce treated as less important. Where did we feel that Croce went wrong? (1) In blurring the historical and empirical differences between the various artistic 'genres', their particular kinds of 'rhetoric', their practical and social objectives; (2) in failing therefore to consider problems of artistic technique (since for him the concrete *construction* of the work had nothing to do with the self-sufficiency of its poetic intuition); (3) in overstressing the part played by emotion and imaginative intuition, and under-rating the elements of calculation, intelligence, technical know-how which are part of the artist's way of working and ought also to be part of the critic's estimate; (4) and finally, because of all this, in restricting critical method to drawing a line between poetry and non-poetry, and classing everything else as inessential 'structure'. On the contrary, what matters in a work like Dante's *Commedia* is precisely these 'left-overs'; for its theological structure, the conventions underlying any medieval artistic allegory of this sort, the range of its characters and concepts bear witness to a whole historical tradition and cultural background. Basing themselves on Croce's method, his followers reduced Dante to nothing but an anthology of poetical lightning flashes, of lyrical moments. We in our turn reacted by devoting ourselves to the history of poetics, to the search for the various conceptions of art needed to grasp all the artistic values of a work, even though it had necessarily to be judged on the basis of the sensibilities of our own time.

A number of contemporary Italian aestheticians have gone beyond Croce in different ways; I would single out Luigi Pareyson's *Estetica* partly because it seems to me the most thorough and successful attempt at systematization since Croce's time, partly because I myself have been influenced by it. But to come back to the main point: all these were reasons attracting me to many aspects of Anglo-American criticism. Thus where the question of technique was concerned I picked up a lot of ideas from those writers who helped me to analyse poetic language from the point of view of its mechanism of communication; I am thinking of the various schools of semantics—specifically I. A. Richards—of the analysis of communication patterns and their effects (for instance Kenneth Burke's book *Counter-statement*), of Charles Morris's semiotics.

In reconsidering 'genres', their particular techniques and their historical development, I learnt a great deal from Anglo-American analyses of plot in novel and play (the names of Francis Fergusson, Warren Beach, Mark Schorer and Joseph Frank spring to mind here, and of course all those who have worked on narrative structure in Joyce). In all these people I could see an impulse towards an *Aristotelian* outlook, towards the kind of rhetorico-structural analysis of which I had had an early example in Poe's *Philosophy of Composition*. Aristotle seemed to be the original master of structural plot analysis; he had distinguished a particular artistic genre capable of communicating a characteristic emotion, tragic catharsis. Yet he made no attempt to clarify the deep-seated causes of this emotion, which were lost somewhere among the roots of Mediterranean folklore, among the rites of Dionysus and the rationalization of Greek medicine. Instead he had constructed a *descriptive*

141

model for understanding the particular strategy of formal elements which triggered off the mechanism of the tragic emotion.

It was with this in mind and in my own manner that I made use of the ideas suggested by the New Criticism or by 'symbolic' aesthetics. Thus what interested me in the critical theory of Philip Wheelwright, for instance, was his analysis of the linguistic sign, of its capacity for *plurisignation*, the use he made of *soft focus*, the principle of *contextualism*; I was interested in the semantic mechanism and the syntactical arrangement which allows a phrase to produce certain precise or ambiguous effects. But the idea that such signs could be referred to archetypal values or to some metaphysical fact seemed to me to belong to cultural history rather than to aesthetics. I look to cultural history to explain why a particular linguistic structure will operate in a given cultural context in such a way that (as Professor Knights put it in these columns, with reference to lyric poetry) 'routine notions and attitudes are broken down, and a new direction of consciousness emerges from the interplay of meanings . . . meanings in which the reader or spectator is involved as a person. . . .' In this way I hold that the formal analysis of a work's structural mechanics (and the working out of constant structural patterns to be found in any work of art) does not lead one to treat the work as *an end in itself* (as with many of the new critics) but serves to provide the instruments by which to understand the relations between work, cultural context and the personality of the writer.

For I hold art (and thus literature too) to be an edifice of values constructed in such a way that everything *preceding* it can be understood through its 'mode of formation', while the mode of formation similarly leads to an understanding of what *results* from it. Because of this, I don't believe that 'formal' consideration of a work means accepting any kind of aesthetic 'formalism' but rather the opposite: the formal approach is the sole way of correctly clarifying relationships between the work and the world of other values.

It was just this that led me to emphasize the historical and relative aspect of the different conceptions of art, and here I have been influenced by another category of reading that has little to do with criticism perhaps but ranks for me quite equally as an Anglo-American cultural influence: I am thinking of the discoveries of cultural anthropology, of 'field-work' designed to trace out *patterns of culture.* My most recent researches into contemporary poetics do in fact represent an attempt to establish models of poetics which would show a profound transformation of our concepts of art to be taking place just now. From Joyce to serial music, from non-figurative painting to the films of Antonioni, the work of art is becoming more and more an *opera aperta,* an open, ambiguous work which instead of a coherent and orderly world of values tends to suggest a 'range' of meanings, a 'field' of possibilities, and to this end calls more and more for active intervention, for an operative choice on the part of reader or viewer. In establishing this model of the *open work* I made considerable use of information theory, another largely Anglo-American influence. And at the same time I tried to relate this aesthetic model to other models which can be identified within the sphere of contemporary culture: from physics with its methodological models, to those of multi-value logic, of psychology, etc. My aim here was to show the unity of the different aspects of the particular cultural moment in which we live. I am not sure, however, that I managed to avoid facile comparisons. And just because of this I have now begun to turn my attention to various structuralist methodologies (from de Saussure's linguistics to Claude Lévi-Strauss's anthropology; at the same time I have always been intrigued by the notion of 'stratified structure' put forward by René Wellek, while the researches of the Russian formalists interest me at present as they also interest him) with a view to solving a particular problem: how to reduce the different cultural manifestations of a single period to precise structural models so as to be able to show what structural patterns they have in common. This does not mean discovering 'ontological' relationships but finding that one can use the same conceptual tools to describe different phenomena.

It is only at this stage, in my view, that one can embark on wider historical analyses and ask about the relations between these more or less similar models and the economic and social bases of a civilization or a period. And it is only on these terms that I feel we can accept the arguments of a Marxism which won't set out naively to establish direct determinist connexions between basic phenomena and those of the superstructure, without taking into account the complex network of influences that embrace the different aspects of a single culture and lead to continual unevenness of development.

I said earlier that I am burdened with one characteristic legacy of Italian aesthetic culture. This is the conviction that such researches do not merely lead to historical relativism but allow one to put forward, if only as a working hypothesis, permanent patterns on which to base a definition of the artistic phenomenon over and above the continual shift of standards. Obviously this is the business of aesthetics and not necessarily of criticism. It struck me that many of the Anglo-American critics who contributed to the last special number of *The Times Literary Supplement* showed a lively concern with a kind of literature which would help to improve our understanding of human experience and of the values which matter to us. My own definition of art, as a form in which values (the 'before' that *precedes* a work's gestation and the 'after' towards which it is directed) merge in structure and acquire importance only in so far as this structure has its own values, means that works of art may convey a scheme of values which would seem negative to me. There are then two possibilities. Either the new order bestowed on them by their artistic form may help me to make contact with them by means of greater sympathy and understanding. Or else on being faced with the work I may grasp the values communicated by it and reject them none the less. In that case I can discuss a work of art on the political and ethical plane, and contest it and refute it precisely because it is a work of art. That is to say that Art is not the Absolute, but a form of activity dialectically related to other activities, other interests, other values. Confronted with it, and in so far as I recognize the validity of the work in question, I can apply my own choice and pick my own masters. There perhaps lies a further and specific task for criticism: to induce choice and discrimination. However severe the technical and structural criteria he professes, anybody reading a work of literature can and should establish emotional and intellectual contact with the world of the author, and make a picture of the man himself and his world. It is quite right that there should be exceptionally sensitive people who communicate this experience of reading in such a way that we can make it our own.

But this is a dialogue between human beings in course of which both our standards of judgment and the demands we make of the work of art are changed. That is why it is in my opinion a good thing that there should, at the same time, be a type of research that sets out to describe and analyse such aesthetic models as they come into being and as they relate to our history.

DÁMASO ALONSO

Towards a Knowledge of Literary Works

⬤◦◦◦◦⬤

C riticism is both a precise and a vague word, precise in as
much as all criticism has as its object the work of art (the
work of literature, to narrow it down to our own field),
vague in every other sense. The chief purpose of that form of
criticism which the public knows best is to tell the multitudes,
who must pick and choose from huge quantities of printed
matter, what they can read and what they should ignore. As
practised by the daily papers criticism must of necessity be
hurried, but from this hasty form of it we can, without ever
leaving the category 'criticism', pass through all the various
stages of deceleration, from criticism in literary reviews down
to thick tomes devoted to the work of a single author, or to a
single book. In this way we not only pass from the hasty and
superficial to the slow and detailed but our very way of looking
at the work in question changes with each type of criticism. The
critic of a daily paper need not do much more than give a few
brief reasons for recommending what he does from among the
new books. Other critics, writing for increasingly limited audiences, want to act as interpreters, to comment on the book, and
explain its beauties or its arguments to their readers. Even at
this level there are many different varieties of critic and of
criticism. The one which interests me most is when the observer
stands before a work of literature filled with the desire to penetrate into its very depths and substance as a living and unique
creation. This being my own approach, my prime concern has
been to ascertain what rational process or magic formula can

help us apprehend the secret of what makes a work of literature as unique as God or myself, and whence it derives the strength that belongs to any literary creation that is intense and original. It goes without saying that for this the first essential is a true work of literature. We are at a far remove from the usual sense of the words 'criticism' and 'work of literature'. This last term we shall restrict to those works which possess, and have preserved through the ages, the permanent ability to attract and hold their readers, and to arouse in them profound emotional reactions: delight, serenity, tenderness, compassion, horror, laughter, and so on. We all know that mere handful of works which can still do this, and will continue to do so in the foreseeable future. It is not that men's idea of them has not changed. To some extent they have a life of their own, a life lived by mankind. *Don Quixote* was what we would call a work of literature right from the start, but for Cervantes's contemporaries it was a sort of splendid farce. For the eighteenth century, and no one shows this better than Fielding, it was virtually an all-embracing history of man. The nineteenth century saw Don Quixote and Sancho as symbolizing the two planes on which we can live our lives, the quest after an ideal and material necessity. The twentieth century, with Unamuno and Papini, has yoked the immortal pair together beneath the light of the same bright madness. This is unimportant: the book's attraction for its readers, and its ability still to arouse deep and original responses in them, have continued unchanged. In the same way mankind has continued through the ages to give fresh meanings to the Homeric epics, to the *Divina Commedia*, to the plays of Shakespeare and so on. They change certainly, but they are alive, and grow more deeply so with time.

Examples such as these are not open to argument, but we cannot restrict the term 'work of literature' to the few works that are truly universal. Each country's literature has its own creations which never lose their interest for succeeding generations, and which other countries are aware of to a greater or lesser extent. But it is lamentably true that every history of literature in every country devotes page after page to works that are totally insipid or throw off only an occasional spark. The academic establishment is tireless in their praise, and from time to time they are reissued, with introductions and notes. A few scholars devote detailed studies to them, which will perhaps be read by half a dozen colleagues scattered round the world, and read solely so that they can disagree with their distant confrère. Unfortunate students, preparing for their examinations, curse the boredom of these highly praised texts, and finally fall asleep over them. The academic establishment is trying to preserve a fiction, because these books do not really exist; they are dead.

What we should like then is to obtain scientific knowledge about 'real' works of literature. Many others have been faced with this same problem, and the question is by now an old one: can one formulate laws for the mental sciences—in our case a hypothetical science of literature—more or less on the model of those of the physical sciences?

Obviously not. Release a stone, any stone or any object, into the void, and it will fall. From the repetition of this phenomenon a law may be induced. But a work of literature, the 'Ode on a Grecian Urn', for example, cannot be defined by what it has in common with other odes. Even after this, and other similar aspects of it, have been exhausted, what constitutes the excitement and interest of the poem will remain as intact and mysterious as before. What we are seeking is the essence of the work, what it contains that makes it the 'Ode on a Grecian Urn', what constitutes its personality so to speak. A work of literature exists by virtue of what is virginal in it, what is uncontaminated and unique in its mode of being.

I have devoted a book to this problem: *Poesía Española: Ensayo de métodos y límites estilísticos*, published in 1950. (Abbreviated German translation entitled *Spanische Dichtung. Versuch über Methoden und Grenzen der Stilistik*. Berne, 1962.) I am still dubious about having used the word, 'estilístico' in the title, because I was working from a conception of the words 'style' and 'stylistic' somewhat different from the usual one. It happens quite frequently that I am wrongly credited with the aims and intentions of the normally accepted sense of the word 'stylistic', which I do not share.

To parody an unfortunate phrase—style *is* the work of literature, because for me style means 'everything'—I would stress that: *everything*—'that gives a literary entity, a book, a writer, an age . . . its individuality'. (See D. Alonso. *La Poesía de San Juan de la Cruz*. 3rd Edition, Madrid, 1958.) Since I have repeated this definition of style on various other occasions I was somewhat alarmed by the idea of 'stylistics' which René Wellek attributes to me in *The Times Literary Supplement* for July 26 (p. 549). Mr. Wellek there takes 'stylistics' to mean the study of 'the sound-stratum (euphony, metre and the like) and the units of meaning (diction, syntax, style)'. But the 'stylistics' which I not only practise but have tried to define and to some extent create is not the study of these things, nor even largely the study of them, but the study of everything which individualizes a work of literature. My efforts have been mainly devoted to trying to redeem 'stylistics' from an exclusive attention to the surface of the work, and directing it towards the conceptual and affective content.

To adopt the terminology which Saussure used for the component parts of the linguistic 'sign', I would distinguish in the literary 'sign' the 'signifier' and the 'signified'. Saussure saw in the signifying acoustic image merely one syllable or a succession of syllables which, within a language, evoke in the mind of the person hearing, reading or pronouncing them, a single definite concept; thus 'arbre' in French evokes the object 'tree'. Unlike Saussure I take into account, in the phonic constitution of a word, not only its syllabic structure but everything that expresses something in real speech: the succession of syllables, intonation, basic tone, intensity, speed, fluency, interruptions and so on. Nor is the 'signified' merely a concept but a complex of conceptual, affective and imaginative elements—the whole intricate current we transmit when we speak. It has moreover to be laid down that we can set no limits to the linear extension of a 'signifier'; a whole poem can be a literary 'sign'. The *Divina Commedia* is a vast 'signifier', as it is also a vast 'signified'.

As far as Saussure, and most of his followers, are concerned, the relationship of the two worlds which meet in speech, the phonic and its mental correlative, is not motivated (there is thus no special reason why 'arbre' should be called 'tree' in English). But one cannot deal with words *in vitro*, or as if they were butterflies impaled in a glass case. Even when a work has been isolated artificially the speaker is aware of a motivation, and if we now consider the case of a poem the whole thing is a motivation of the links between the signifying sound and the 'signified'. It is this motivation that gave birth to it, and the links are reforged each time the poem is read.

This motivation which presides over the act of speech, and is the repeated illusion of the speaker (illusion is also a reality), is even more intense in literature, and especially poetry. The whole purpose of my book was to study the poetic 'sign' and the connexions between the 'signifier' and the 'signified'.

To study a poem, or any piece of literature, stylistically, means understanding it as a 'sign', that is to say, in the connexion or equation which it establishes between the signifying element and the message signified. As I see 'stylistics' it is essential that one's examination of a work should be able to start equally well from the external arrangement of the words as from their conceptual or affective content. In many cases one need be in no doubt as to which course to choose; some poets—Petrarch or Góngora for instance—offer one so much data in the way of 'signifying' that they seem to be inviting one to start there. With others the same approach is doomed at least to disappointment, and the investigator will do well to direct his attention to the message signified, as with St. John of the Cross or Donne. This approach is almost always more difficult. It depends at times that one penetrate deep into mental worlds or, in another direction, into details of biography and history. Most often one's analysis needs to fluctuate between these two extreme positions.

TOWARDS A KNOWLEDGE OF LITERARY WORKS

There can be no doubt that the analysis of a piece of writing seems more immediately practicable from the point of view of the signifying sound. Here, in the work itself, we have the phonic elements, audible, measurable, even capable of being recorded in various ways. The world of the 'signified' on the other hand is profound and elusive, for although it is relatively simple to establish where a poet has obtained his general ideas from (philosophical and political systems, etc.), or how he has developed psychologically (story of his life, landscapes, poems read, etc.) it is still extremely difficult to assess how and by what stages these elements have cohered into the 'signified'. We can imagine it as a very complex mass of thought, emotion and imagination that suddenly begins to move and mould itself into something. We seem to be at the instant preceding the poem. A few moments more and we shall have before us the resplendent shape of a new-born child—the creative work of literature. The loftiest aim of 'stylistics' is to explain how this bridge is built between the 'signified' as it emerges into being and the 'signifier'—how in fact the 'sign' is created.

This too is the very point where it fails—hence the limitations of my title. 'Stylistics' will always remain a desperate aspiration towards a science of literature, an imperfect science, if I may be allowed the term. For there is no way of penetrating into the 'signified' by scientific techniques, unless we have previously grasped it by intuition. This means that the literary analyst must be, before all else, a reader, a reader with subtle and flexible responses—a quality alas often lacking in literary analysts. Once the 'thing signified' has been apprehended by intuition, then indeed it is possible to re-apprehend it by analysis, that is to say that the scientific process must be controlled and guided by intuition.

Let us consider Fray Luis de León's 'Oda a Salinas'. Fray Luis de León's entire life was a mystical aspiration that was for ever impeded by his combative temperament and by long years spent in the prisons of the Inquisition. His poetry is one long cry, now of desolation, now of protest. The poet has glimpsed

151

the Elysian fields, but he looks on them not with the joy of mystical union but the bitterness of exile. There is only one ode, the 'Ode to Salinas', where he expresses fleetingly the joys of union. He achieves it through music, for the short space of two verses. In my book I elected to examine this ode from the point of view of the 'thing signified', to see how the elements of the poet's life and thought flowed together into it. Starting from the Pythagorean ideas about the harmony of numbers he ascends from the music of the earth to that of the spheres and the universe, to God, the great musician who causes it to sound. The result is an ascent, a ladder, such as is found in mystics of every age, based on an obviously Platonic model. St. John of the Cross ends his poems at the moment of supreme joy, when he can no longer find words for his love and his voice dies away into a stammer. With Fray Luis this great joy lasts barely ten lines and is at once replaced in the poem by his habitual feelings of exile. Thus, from considerations arising out of the 'thing signified' we can manage to guess something of the internal structure of the poem. By moving on to the 'signifying sound' we shall be able to witness the moment when the literary 'sign' is created.

Fray Luis is one of the greatest of Spanish Horatians. From his mentor he took, among other things, the pattern of climax and anti-climax in the ode form. We can now understand what had to happen in the 'Ode to Salinas'; the double conceptual structure—the Platonic aesthetic and the idea of mystical ascent by stages—reached a peak, followed by a descent, aggravated in Fray Luis's case by the terrible experiences of his life. This structure, with its twin conceptual bases and its biographical background, took its natural shape from the sequence of climax and anti-climax which Fray Luis had learnt from Horace. The thought and the lived experience only manage to become the 'thing signified' at that creative moment when the wonderful equation is realized: 'Sign'='signified'+'signifier'.

Most literary investigation in this world of ours is not applied directly to the work of literature. It consists in amassing mountains of paper—nearly all our biographical studies, books with titles like 'The Philosophy of . . . such and such a poet', many studies of comparative literature and sources, books belonging to that special class of source-seeking which Curtius began with his *topoi*, and so on. Need I say that these books are often magnificent, that they are absolutely necessary, that a great deal of my time is devoted to the same kind of researches? What I want is not that such work should be abandoned, but that we should introduce a little precision and clarity into our thinking, that we should know what it is that we are really doing, that we should not confuse work that is very valuable for the history of culture, even of literary culture, with the one thing with which we are here centrally concerned—the study of the work itself, as the object of our scientific inquiry.

Let us return to our example. To establish what Fray Luis de León's ideas were, to assemble, from among his many writings in Latin and Spanish, the traces of Pythagorean teachings, to track down the ideas of Plato or the influence of the Christian mystics, or the imprint left by his biblical studies, or, in another direction, to discern the ups and downs of his life, his struggles with the University, his spirited defence against the Inquisition, all these are vital activities. They are both an addition to our knowledge of Spanish culture in the sixteenth century and also necessary as an aid to studying the true object of literary analysis —the poem. All this is necessary, yes, but it is now time to turn our attention to what is essential: the nature of the poem, the work itself, that delectable creature which allows itself to be possessed by our intuitive understanding, yet proves so elusive to our attempts at scientific analysis. Herein lies the problem. I did not presume to solve it in my book; my intention was merely to pose it in all its urgent and dramatic necessity.

JAN KOTT

Angles on Poles and Saxons

———————————◆⊃◦⊂◆———————————

P rofessionals, of course, read everything. There are specialists on spiders, on ballistics during the Punic Wars and on
Anglo-Saxon literary criticism. The student who is preparing his yearly work or thesis on Faulkner, Joyce or Eliot is
required by his professor to read everything, or almost everything, that has been written by the author he has chosen, at least
everything in English. There are also avid and scrupulous readers
of English and American literary criticism among translators and
readers for publishing houses. It is part of their professional duty.

I think, though, that the questions posed by *The Times Literary
Supplement* are concerned, mainly, with something different: the
real place of Anglo-Saxon literary criticism in the modern intellectual life of my country and its influence on Polish literary
criticism. In order to answer such a question, however, we must
first of all agree on what we understand by the term 'literary
criticism'.

If we mean literary criticism in the literal and narrow sense,
that is books or articles by writers about other writers, or even
non-academic literary history, I can say quite conscientiously
that the influence of Anglo-Saxon literary criticism is very small,
and its effect on intellectual currents and discussions appears to
be equally negligible. I think, though, that of the two words
'literary criticism' it is possible to place the accent on the word
'criticism' and to treat the word 'literary' widely and freely;
that we must consider also that literary genre, or rather that
branch of writing, which has always been one of the most charac-

teristic features of Anglo-Saxon literature. I am thinking of the essay; not only of the essay that is purely literary but also of the philosophical, social, and even the scientific essay, in which literature is only one of many subjects of analysis and criticism. Understood in this way, Anglo-Saxon critically-minded writing has affected the intellectual life of Poland on many occasions, and continues to affect it now. In this case a short look at history is essential and also, perhaps, quite interesting.

It will probably surprise the majority of readers to know that the English essay on literature and manners played a very important role during the Polish Enlightenment. The most prominent periodical of the Polish Enlightenment was *Monitor*, which was published in Warsaw from 1765. *Monitor* was both a simple imitation and also to a great extent an adaptation of successive yearbooks of the English *The Spectator*. Of course adaptations were carried out at this time exclusively through French translations. Translations of Defoe, Swift and Fielding which were published at this time were likewise taken from the French. Steele and Addison taught the backward Polish nobility respect for law, thrift, common sense and other bourgeois virtues. Bacon and Locke, who were time and time again quoted in the journalism of the Polish Enlightenment, were two of the first teachers of empirical thought and tolerance.

English philosophers and economists became for the second time the teachers of that same still backward Polish nobility a hundred years later, at the beginning of the second half of the nineteenth century. This time John Stuart Mill and, especially, Spencer were the highest authorities, which were quoted and invoked by the first Polish worshippers of the steam engine and capitalist progress. In Polish literature this period bears the name of 'positivism'. Mill, Spencer and, besides them and perhaps to a still greater extent, Darwin were quoted incessantly in journalism and literary criticism. They created a school of thought and argument in which utilitarianism was the highest ideal, and the rules and customs of daily life as well as literary genres evolved happily and beneficially.

At the turn of the nineteenth and twentieth centuries there were three encounters with English thought which I consider particularly far-reaching. The most prominent literary critic of that time and one of its greatest personalities was Stanislaw Brzozowski who, in a way that was extremely violent but always basically constructive, battled with the philosophy of Marx and Sorel, of Mach and the pragmatists. Towards the end of his short but tempestuous life he drew quite close to Roman Catholicism, and it was then that the very powerful writings of Newman began to affect him. The stern and intellectual Catholicism of Newman was contrasted by Brzozowski with the traditional, comfortable and sentimental Catholicism of Poland.

Ruskin, who was many times translated during his lifetime, is quoted by the modernist poets and by the more refined of the socialists. In Poland he is considered one of the champions of new aesthetic sensibility, and especially of the new interest in regional art and handicraft.

Most astonishing of all was the third encounter, in this case an encounter in the literal sense of the word. At the beginning of the century a young enthusiast of the theatre from Cracow, Leon Schiller, met E. G. Craig in Florence and was fascinated by his personality and ideas. He even published in Craig's journal *The Mask* which was edited and put out by Craig a skit on Stanislaw Wyspiański, the Polish poet, painter, dramatist and scenographer of the modernist period who was, as was specifically demanded by Craig, one of the first universal artists of the theatre.

Leon Schiller is still the most prominent theorist of the Polish stage and is to this day unsurpassed as a director, especially of Polish romantic monumental drama. Throughout all his life Schiller remained true to the cult of Craig and has engrained him into the Polish theatre. In the period between the two wars Craig was probably better known and esteemed in Poland than in his own country. The cult of Craig has remained alive until the present day. I spent this past winter in Vence, where Craig has resided for some years. A couple of my young students who were interested in theatrical criticism wrote to me from Poland and asked me to communicate to Craig their New Year greetings and also their deepest admiration.

This meeting of Craig and Schiller in Florence is one of the most important dates in the history of the modern theatre in Poland. The fascination of these two men must have been mutual, since this grand old man, more than ninety years old, when I introduced myself to him as a theatre critic from Poland, sang me a song which he had heard from Schiller more than half a century before.

After the First World War I must mention three English writers whose essays and reflections have had an extremely lasting effect on criticism and intellectual life in Poland. The first of these was Chesterton whose ideas, like those of Newman in his time, were contrasted with good-natured Polish Catholicism. Only in the last years before the war did intellectual Catholics in Poland yield to the influence of Maritain, whereupon Chesterton receded into the background.

The second writer whose influence was greatly felt in the period before the Second World War was Wells. A great admirer and popularizer of Wells was Antoni Słonimski, one of Poland's greatest humorists, a poet and writer of comedies, whose journalistic writings have shaped the opinions of a considerable part of the Warsaw intelligentsia. For the third time, characteristically, an attempt was made to adapt to Poland the English philosophy of common sense. Through all the differences of successive ages Addison, Spencer and Wells were for 200 years the teachers in Poland of a very similar type of thought and, roughly, of these same values: liberalism and tolerance, belief in social teaching, conviction in the progress of civilization. Beside Wells great influence, especially among the bourgeois intelligentsia of Warsaw, has been exercised by the books of Bertrand Russell which have been translated and published many times. It is characteristic that this influence was revived during the period of the 'Polish October', when for the first time after the war the writing of sceptical sketches was resumed.

We have now reached the present day. There are a couple of points, though, which I must add. It is impossible to speak accurately of the influence of modern Anglo-Saxon criticism and essays, without first taking note, though briefly, of the great advance which has occurred in knowledge of the English language and of American literature. Before 1939 German, French and Russian were far better known in Poland than English. During the partitions German and Russian were the state languages, compulsory in schools and administration; a knowledge of French was long recognized as a proof of intellectual refinement and social polish. The average intelligent Pole, if he could not speak them, at least could read freely in two foreign languages, usually French and German. Even in my literary generation French is decidedly better known than English.

During the Second World War this situation was drastically changed. A large number of Poles at that time found themselves in Great Britain, or else formed part of those units of the Polish Army which fought under British leadership. Certain modern Polish writers are now in emigration, and among them many of the most prominent are in England and America. The influence of Anglo-Saxon criticism on this group is, of course, incomparably stronger and would entail separate treatment.

It is also worth mentioning the emergence of a small but characteristic group of young Anglo-Polish writers who are entirely bilingual. Among them are people who had time to begin or finish school in Poland under German occupation and attended university in England. It is this group which is a natural bridge between Anglo-Saxon thought and literary life in Poland. The knowledge of English has also grown immensely among the Polish youth of today, both among students of the exact sciences and among students of the humanities, literature and art.

The position of Anglo-Saxon literature in the publishing market has also changed. Not only is it more widely read and translated but it has a stronger and more active influence on literary life. This is particularly true of American literature.

After 1955, in which year the flood gates were opened, the great American 'lost generation' quartet, Steinbeck, Caldwell, Hemingway and Faulkner, was very soon made accessible to the Polish reader, and almost all their books have become best-sellers. The last two especially, Faulkner and Hemingway, have a great influence on the style, writing technique and, to a certain extent, on the world outlook of the young generation of writers.

Among English writers the influence of Conrad is maintained continually, and he has not ceased to fascinate all literary generations in Poland, both old and young. A well-known critic was once asked who was the greatest Polish novelist; his answer was, 'Joseph Conrad, unfortunately!' Conrad's nearness to us and apartness, the choice which he made, and what in him is Polish and what English—all this has been the subject of several books and numerous discussions in Poland.

The interest in Conrad and in the modern American novel leads in some measure to an interest in criticism. I think, though, that this interest should not be overestimated. In the long run French literary journals are read far more widely in Poland than English or American. It must be clearly stated that although in the readership market the Anglo-Saxon novel is predominant, in other branches of literature, such as poetry and the theatre, among western literatures the French influence is still the most marked. This is true of all criticism, but especially of philosophical and ideological criticism, which of all countries enjoy probably their greatest popularity in France and Poland. Criticism begins to have an intensive effect on literature and intellectual life when it creates its own language and system of values. Sartre and Camus created such a language and their influence cannot be compared with any other.

Of the English literary journals the most known and read in intellectual circles are *The Observer*, *The Times Literary Supplement* and *Encounter*. This fact determines how well any particular literary critic is known. Among the best known are Cyril Connolly, V. S. Pritchett, Raymond Mortimer and Philip Toynbee. In the same circles the *New Yorker* is the most popular

American journal. Of American critics Edmund Wilson and Dwight Macdonald have their admirers.

In Poland there is great interest in theatrical life and the stage, and especially in the English theatre. In consequence there is an interest in English theatrical criticism. The name of Kenneth Tynan is well known in Poland and his articles are often quoted in the theatrical press.

Today, though, the most important encounters with Anglo-Saxon thought exceed the narrow bounds of literary criticism in the strict sense. My readers will perhaps be surprised to hear that Professor Roman Jakobson of Harvard University, the well-known Russian scholar and literary theoretician, had a definite effect on the emergence of a new direction in literary research, which concentrated on mathematical methods and on the use of language and information theory. Even before the war there was keen interest among young students of the humanities in Russian formalism and structural methods in linguistics and poetry. Jakobson's theoretical work on language as communication and on poetic styles as a definite code system began to interest critics as well, and it became known far outside normal academic circles. It can be said with a certain, though slight, exaggeration that Jakobson is the patron of the young school of poetic criticism in Poland.

The links between Polish and Anglo-Saxon sociology were particularly strong even long before the war. In this connexion I should mention the names of Malinowski and Znaniecki. During the last couple of years a good part of Polish literary criticism has been concerned with the question of 'mass culture'. The names of many American sociologists who work on this problem have been mentioned by literary critics, who have been partly reporting their views and partly arguing with them. American sociology has also influenced questionnaire research, which has been taken up again in Poland. Sadly, all this is very far from literary criticism, but this is precisely the point about Polish literary criticism: that it is concerned not only with literature, and that it is involved with the most varied forms of intellectual activity and experiment in many spheres of life.

In this context one more name must be mentioned. Two books of Norbert Wiener on cybernetics have been translated and have confirmed the undoubted influence of modern literary criticism on language and the world of ideas.

I think that these examples have given some idea of what the distinctive characteristics of Polish literary criticism are based on. The story is often told of the professor of zoology from Warsaw or Cracow who was asked to an international congress of scientists and read a paper on 'The Elephant and the Polish Question'. Literary criticism is a little like that scientist. It is Marxist, liberal or Catholic; it is interested in existentialism, structuralism, science fiction, information theory and many problems which do not always have much in common with literature. But this universalism in Polish literary criticism is, in fact, only an appearance. It is very deeply engaged in the Poland of the present day, even when it is speaking of it in the language of existentialism or is discussing the experiments of American research into mass culture. Nevertheless, as a result of these very experiments it appears that Polish criticism has many new and important things to say, even for the reader from abroad. In the dramatic changes of the past ten years Polish criticism has played an important and on many occasions a pioneer role. It has ceased to be provincial. In all the dialogues between East and West the voice of Polish criticism has always been independent and is often worthy of notice.

In the nineteenth century, a period of little freedom, literature was often called the conscience of the people. In the same period criticism in its turn was thought to be the conscience of literature. The job of criticism was to coax and persuade literature to fulfil its national and social duties. According to these ideas literature had to be didactic and criticism doubly didactic.

I think that this sort of traditional burden, which is never fully overcome, can best explain the differences between Anglo-Saxon and Polish literary criticism. It is, doubtless, a limitation but it is at the same time a strength of literary criticism in Poland. Thanks to it this criticism is never entirely professional and is rarely confined to an elite. It is fed not by literature alone but also by historical experience.

Notes on Contributors

Dámaso Alonso. Born 1898. Professor of Romance Philology, Madrid University. Author of numerous works on Spanish poetry, ranging from *Poetas españoles contemporaneos* (1918) to *Gongora y el Polifemo* (1961).

Roland Barthes. Born 1915. Professor at the Centre Nationale de la Recherche Scientifique. His best-known book is *Sur Racine* (1962); he was also one of the earliest theoreticians of the new French novel.

Emilio Cecchi. Born 1884. Well-known Italian critic. His many and varied works include *Scrittori Inglesi e Americani* (1935), *Florentiner Plastik des Quattrocento* (1951) and *Periplo dell' Africa* (1954).

Umberto Eco. Born 1932. 'Libero docente' in Aesthetics at the University of Turin. Has done considerable research in contemporary poetics, and in the stylistics of popular literature including comic books. His best-known book is *Opera Aperta* (1963).

Richard Hoggart. Born 1918. Professor of English, Birmingham University. Amongst his publications is the influential study of popular literature, *The Uses of Literacy* (1957).

Graham Hough. Born 1908. Professor of English Literature, Cambridge University. His works include *The Last Romantics* (1949) and a study of D. H. Lawrence, *The Dark Sun* (1957).

Jan Kott. Born 1914. Professor of the History of Polish Literature, Warsaw University. A volume of his essays was published in a French translation, under the title *Shakespeare notre contemporain,* in 1963.

F. R. Leavis. Born 1895. Fellow of Downing College, Cambridge. Editor of *Scrutiny* (1932–53) and author of a number

163

of influential critical works including *Revaluation* (1936), *The Great Tradition* (1948), and *D. H. Lawrence, Novelist* (1955).

Harry Levin. Born 1912. Irving Babbitt Professor of Comparative Literature at Harvard University. His more recent publications include *Contexts of Criticism* (1957), *The Power of Blackness* (1958) and *The Gates of Horn* (1963).

L. C. Knights. Born 1906. Winterstoke Professor of English at Bristol University. His works include *Drama and Society in the Age of Jonson* (1937) and *Explorations* (1946).

Hans Mayer. Born 1907. Until recently Professor of the History of German Literature, at Leipzig University; now lives in West Germany. He has written, amongst other books, *Von Lessing bis Thomas Mann* (1959) and *Bertolt Brecht und die Tradition* (1961).

Raymond Picard. Born 1917. Professor in the Faculty of Letters in the University of Lille.

W. W. Robson. Born 1923. Fellow of Lincoln College, Oxford. His publications include *Byron as Poet*, the British Academy Chatterton Lecture on an English Poet for 1957.

Emil Staiger. Born 1908. Professor of German Literature at Zurich University. His important works include *Die Kunst der Interpretation* (1951) and *Stilwandel* (1963).

George Steiner. Born 1929. Fellow of Churchill College, Cambridge. He has published *Tolstoy or Dostoevsky* (1960) and *The Death of Tragedy* (1961).

John Wain. Born 1925. Novelist, poet and critic. His best-known novel is *Hurry on Down!* (1953).

René Wellek. Born 1903. Professor of Slavic and Comparative Literature at Yale University. Author of *Theory of Literature* (1949) (with Austin Warren) and *A History of Modern Criticism* (1955).

Index

165

INDEX

Salinger, J. D., 29
Santayana, G., 52
Sartre, J. P., 69, 115, 123; on
  Baudelaire, 104; influence of,
  in Poland, 159
Schiller, F., 108, 109, 132
Schiller, Leon, 156
Schlagfiguren, 131, 132, 133
Schorer, Mark, 141
Schücking, L. L., 45
Scott, Sir Walter, as reviver of
  Middle Ages, 61
Scrutiny, 42, 80, 93, 94, 95,
  163
Selincourt, E. de, 117
Semantics, 15; *see* Barthes, Eco,
  Richardo
'Separation of powers', 108–15
Shakespeare, W., 24, 25, 46, 49,
  63–4, 66, 71, 73, 74, 79, 80,
  101, 102, 104, 128, 147; mis-
  anthropy of, 58; Grabbe's de-
  nigration of, 108; Lessing on,
  109; Henry IV, 50; *King Lear*,
  35, 77, 78; Johnson on *King
  Lear*, 63–4; *Merchant of Venice*,
  57, 79, 112; *Venus and Adonis*,
  79
Shelley, P. B., *A Defence of Poetry*,
  116
Sievers, Rutz and Nohl, analysis
  of sounds by, 132
Sidney, Sir Philip, 56
'Signs', literary, 149, 150
'Sincerity' of author, 12, 55–6
Slonimski, Antoni, 157
Smollett, Tobias, 112
'Soft focus' (Philip Wheel-
  wright), 142
Sophocles, 130
Sorel, 156 G.,
Spectator, The, 155

Spencer, Herbert, influence of, in
  Poland, 155, 157
Spenser, Edmund, 28
Staiger, Emil, 13–14, 130–7, 164;
  Goethe, 134; *Grundbegriffe der
  Poetik*, 137, 164; *Die Kunst der
  Interpretation*, 137, 164; *Die
  Zeit als Einbildungskraft des
  Dichters*, 130, 133, 137; *Stil-
  wandel*, 137
Stanislavsky, 74
Starobinski, J., 124
Steiner, George, 13, 21–3, 111,
  112, 121, 164
Stendhal, 28, 103
Sterne, L., 112
Stevenson, R. L., 118
'Stratified structure', 143; *see*
  Wellek, R.
Structural plot analysis, 138 seqq.
Structuralism in French criticism,
  124
Style as 'everything', 149
Stylistics, 11, 15, 148 seqq.
Sublime, Treatise on the (Monk),
  118
Substance analysis, in French
  criticism, 124
'Suspension of disbelief', 35–6, 51
Swift, J., 58; in Poland, 155
Symbolic language of poetry, 80

Taine, H., 124; and Hegel, 119
'Tangible Results' (TLS leader),
  91
Tate, Nahum, *King Lear* version
  by, 64
Theory: emerging from history,
  47; enemies of, 40
Theory of Literature, see Wellek
  and Warren
Thomas, Dylan, 53

173